Let the Biscuits Burn

Cultivating Real-Life Hospitality *in a* World Craving Connection

Abby Kuykendall

An Imprint of Thomas Nelson

Let the Biscuits Burn

Copyright © 2025 by Abby Kuykendall

All rights reserved. No portion of this book may be reproduced, stored in a retrieval system, or transmitted in any form or by any means—electronic, mechanical, photocopy, recording, scanning, or other—except for brief quotations in critical reviews or articles, without the prior written permission of the publisher.

Published by Nelson Books, an imprint of Thomas Nelson, 501 Nelson Place, Nashville, TN 37214, USA. Nelson Books and Thomas Nelson are registered trademarks of HarperCollins Christian Publishing, Inc.

The author is represented by Alive Literary Agency, www.aliveliterary.com.

Thomas Nelson titles may be purchased in bulk for educational, business, fundraising, or sales promotional use. For information, please email SpecialMarkets@ThomasNelson.com.

Unless otherwise noted, Scripture quotations are taken from the Holy Bible, New International Version®, NIV®. Copyright © 1973, 1978, 1984, 2011 by Biblica, Inc.® Used by permission of Zondervan. All rights reserved worldwide. www.zondervan.com. The "NIV" and "New International Version" are trademarks registered in the United States Patent and Trademark Office by Biblica, Inc.® Scripture quotations marked ESV are taken from the ESV® Bible (The Holy Bible, English Standard Version®). Copyright © 2001 by Crossway, a publishing ministry of Good News Publishers. All rights reserved. Scripture quotations marked KJV are taken from the King James Version. Public domain. Scripture quotations marked MSG are taken from *The Message*. Copyright © 1993, 2002, 2018 by Eugene H. Peterson. Used by permission of NavPress. All rights reserved. Represented by Tyndale House Publishers, Inc. Scripture quotations marked NASB are taken from the (NASB®) New American Standard Bible®. Copyright © 1960, 1971, 1977, 1995, 2020 by The Lockman Foundation. Used by permission. All rights reserved. www.lockman. org. Scripture quotations marked NLT are taken from the Holy Bible, New Living Translation. Copyright © 1996, 2004, 2015 by Tyndale House Foundation. Used by permission of Tyndale House Publishers, Carol Stream, Illinois 60188. All rights reserved. Scripture quotations marked TPT are taken from The Passion Translation®. Copyright © 2017, 2018, 2020 by Passion & Fire Ministries, Inc. Used by permission. All rights reserved. ThePassionTranslation.com.

Without limiting the exclusive rights of any author, contributor or the publisher of this publication, any unauthorized use of this publication to train generative artificial intelligence (AI) technologies is expressly prohibited. HarperCollins also exercise their rights under Article 4(3) of the Digital Single Market Directive 2019/790 and expressly reserve this publication from the text and data mining exception.

HarperCollins Publishers, Macken House, 39/40 Mayor Street Upper, Dublin 1, D01 C9W8, Ireland (https://www.harpercollins.com)

Library of Congress Cataloging-in-Publication Data

Names: Kuykendall, Abby, 1989- author
Title: Let the biscuits burn : cultivating real-life hospitality in a world craving connection / Abby Kuykendall.
Description: Nashville, Tennessee : Nelson Books, [2025] | Summary: "Founder of A Table Top Affair and author of The Living Table cookbook, Abby Kuykendall offers an encouraging resource for the hesitant host, with practical advice and biblical inspiration to navigate the beautiful challenges and profound rewards of welcoming others into your home and around your table"-- Provided by publisher.
Identifiers: LCCN 2025014449 (print) | LCCN 2025014450 (ebook) | ISBN 9781400252398 paperback | ISBN 9781400252480 ebook
Subjects: LCSH: Hospitality--Religious aspects--Christianity
Classification: LCC BV4647.H67 K89 2025 (print) | LCC BV4647.H67 (ebook) | DDC 177 /.1--dc23/eng/20250613
LC record available at https://lccn.loc.gov/2025014449
LC ebook record available at https://lccn.loc.gov/2025014450

Printed in the United States of America
25 26 27 28 29 LBC 5 4 3 2 1

To my grandmothers, GrandMary and GrandMolly.

Thank you both for showing me what it means to open my door, pull out a chair, and invite people in to love on them with the love of Christ.

Contents

Introduction vii

Chapter 1: Community Matters 1

Part 1: The Preparation

Chapter 2: Unpacking Hospitality 19
Chapter 3: The Spiritual Discipline of Hospitality 31
Chapter 4: Preparing Your Heart 45

Part 2: The Invitation

Chapter 5: The Excuse You're Making 67
Chapter 6: Go Ahead and Let the Biscuits Burn 89
Chapter 7: The Intentional Invitation 109
Chapter 8: Habitual Hospitality 129

Contents

Part 3: The Transformation

Chapter 9: The Great Invite 145

Chapter 10: Serving Others Without Burning Out ... 161

Chapter 11: The Legacy of Your Table 185

Conclusion: Let's Do the Next Hard Thing 199

Liturgy for Your Heart 203

Table Tips 207

Acknowledgments 223

Notes 225

About the Author 228

Introduction

I have French doors on the front of my house with windowpanes on the top half, so I can clearly see anything and everything outside. Imagine you have just knocked on my door. My dogs would greet you with the most welcoming of barks. Baylor and Mowgli are papillons by genetics but German shepherds at heart. Shortly following their greeting, I would come barreling around the corner with a smile on my face, opening the door and embracing even the newest of friends with a bear hug.

Welcome. Friend, you have found a place where you belong.

Doesn't that feel good? The open door, the warm embrace, the welcome. It's what we all long for, and it's also what God created us to provide. But sometimes the open door, the hug, and that "I'm so glad you are here" are hard to offer, making hospitality seem daunting and unmanageable. Our lives can get hectic, and our homes can become a bit of

Introduction

a disaster zone. Let's be real: Takeout can be a lifesaver on those busy days. Cooking for others? Forget it!

Suppose you find yourself in that space of not knowing how to do this thing called hospitality or even where to start. You are in good company. I'm glad you are here. Because I've been there; I've felt the insecurities around inviting people over and the doubt the Enemy places on my heart as I begin to set the table. The good thing is that we serve a good God who wants to help us overcome those insecurities, say no to the Enemy, and open our home, discovering a new intimacy with him and a deeper connection with his people. Over the next few pages, I pray you are encouraged and excited about the journey the Lord is going to take you on.

The Journey Starts Here

If you picked up this book, I'm guessing it's because you aren't feeling too confident in your hospitality skills. You might have even read the title and said, "Yup! That's me. I burn the biscuits." I'm right there with you!

I recently watched *Martha* on Netflix, the documentary about Martha Stewart, and it was both inspiring and convicting; Martha's story is one of unparalleled drive and accomplishment.[1] Yet beneath the layers of perfection she presented to the world, I couldn't help but feel the weight of the pressure she carried. Her ability to create immaculate tablescapes and her insistence on every detail being flawless left me wondering, *At what cost?* While she built an

Introduction

empire, her life also mirrored the burden many of us feel—this constant need to prove our worth through doing things "right." But what happens when the pursuit of perfection overtakes the joy we are meant to experience? What happens to our hearts when the table becomes a stage rather than a sanctuary?

For so many of us the idea of hospitality has become entangled with a performance mindset. It's not just about inviting someone over; it's about making sure every detail aligns with a certain standard. While watching Martha's story, I saw how the pursuit of excellence can unintentionally build walls rather than bridges. Perfectionism, while alluring, can isolate us. It tells us the table has to look a certain way, the food must be extraordinary, and the atmosphere must feel effortless—but in striving for all that, we miss the point: the joy that should fill the table. Joy is replaced instead with anxiety, and the connections we hope to build are overshadowed by our internal fears of not being enough.

This documentary prompted me to think deeply about what God intended the table to be. The Bible shows us again and again that the table isn't a place for perfection; it's a place for connection, rest, and even surrender. Jesus sat at tables with people society deemed unworthy. He broke bread with sinners, tax collectors, and fishermen—not because their tables were Instagram-worthy but because he knew the table is where hearts are opened. It's a place of meeting, not performing. God designed the table to be a space where we can leave our burdens behind and find deep, soul-level communion with him and others.

Introduction

God isn't coming to critique your burnt biscuits or mismatched plates. He's coming to meet you right where you are. The beauty of the gospel is that it frees us from the lie that we have to earn approval or prove our worth. The table is not where we showcase our best; it's where we bring our honest, imperfect selves and trust that God will fill in the gaps.

This book will help you retrain your heart and mind to embrace that freedom. Together, we'll shift our focus away from the centerpiece and toward the people in the seats. We'll learn how to let the biscuits burn, laugh about it, and keep serving, because what matters isn't the meal but the memories. You'll discover that hospitality isn't about achieving some unattainable standard; it's about making space for others, even when it's messy.

As you navigate this book and read these pages, I encourage you to let go of any fears or insecurities you may have about inviting people into your home. Your home does not have to be perfect, your meal does not have to be gourmet, and your hosting skills do not have to be flawless. All you need is a heart that is willing to open up to others and a desire to create a space of love and acceptance.

This book is a journey—not toward some domestic sainthood like the hosts of the Food Network but toward rediscovering the hospitality hidden within you. It's a gentle nudge to embrace the imperfection that makes you uniquely beautiful, to extend a hand of welcome despite the shakiness in your voice. We will explore the beauty of hospitality and how it can transform our lives and the lives of those around us. I'll share funny stories from when I was learning

Introduction

to cultivate a heart for hospitality and what I've learned from the experiences of others. My hope is that by the end of this journey, you will feel empowered to open up your heart and your home to others, just as Christ has opened up his heart to us and invited us into his home.

Let's lean into the grace God offers. Let's reclaim the table as a place of rest, love, and connection. You don't have to be Martha Stewart to be a good host. In fact, the less you strive for perfection, the more room you make for joy. This is the heart of hospitality: an open-handed invitation to experience God's love and share it with others. Let's burn the biscuits together and watch how God uses even our imperfections to create something beautiful.

Chapter 1
• • • • • •
Community Matters

Have you ever had an aha moment? You know, the kind that knocks your breath out and affirms you simultaneously? It's humbling when you're provided this constructive direction instead of being reprimanded. In the moment all you can feel is the goose bumps climbing your arms and the hair on your neck standing straight up, and the only thing I want to do in these moments is crawl in a hole and not come out until the year 2080. Wait. Is that even going to be a year? Well, if it is, I will still be in that hole.

I had one of those aha moments in March 2010 when I was a junior at Ouachita Baptist University. I still remember where I was sitting, what I was doing, and who was providing this direction.

Let the Biscuits Burn

I was living in a single room on a hall with my social club sisters, in a not-so-nice dorm. (Remember, I was at a Baptist university. Like many other small Baptist schools in the South, we didn't have national sororities; we had social clubs.*)

While I ended up enjoying the extra space, you can imagine how I had initially felt when no one asked me to be their roommate. I lived in the consolation prize: the single room at the end of the hall—close enough to be near the action but not in the action.

I mostly found myself alone, trying to fill my cup in every way possible. I had grown up sheltered in a small town; this was the year my eyes were opened. I did all the college things one can do at a small Christian university in a dry county in south Arkansas. While my social club sisters were involved in discipleship groups and serving the community, I was planning the next party and enjoying my older, more "sophisticated" friends. Day by day I was falling further from Jesus and who he designed me to be. I was trying my best to create a community but in all the wrong ways.

Halfway through the spring semester, we had to select our roommates and preferred dorm for the following year. Junior and senior year you could request the "bougie" dorms, which had quads of four rooms joined by a communal living room. I dreaded this process as much as some kids

---

* This was also the dorm my dad stayed in when he was a football player at OBU in the late 1970s, and if I'm not mistaken, that was one of only three years that the dorm was not used by football players. *Gross* is an understatement. But we made the most of it with our futons and string lights!

dread picking teams on the playground. Remember, nobody had chosen me the previous year; I had to live alone, and it was not fun.

Therefore, I was not looking forward to this conversation with my friends. Would I be living alone again? Was I even good enough to have a roommate? Maybe I just wasn't a good friend. All these questions permeated my brain, and as I look back at them now, I know that was the Enemy trying to keep me from the good God had planned.

But then something happened that I will never forget. Three of my friends sat me down and asked me to be their fourth roommate. I remember thinking that something must have happened to their first choice of a fourth, but that was okay! I jumped at the chance to live in what I deemed the premium campus suite. This next year was going to be different, and I was stoked.

But then the aha moment came.

Their faces got solemn, and I knew we were about to have a heart-to-heart about something I had been avoiding for quite some time. The Holy Spirit had been trying to have this conversation with me for months, and I had not been listening. So he enlisted friends to confront me and graciously love me through constructive direction.

They asked me about my walk with Jesus. They asked me about the habits I was creating and the decisions I had been making. I was embarrassed. I knew I had not been making good decisions and that God had called me to live differently, but I had been avoiding that conviction, trying to fill the void with what the world deemed fun.

That conversation felt like it lasted a lifetime, but in

retrospect was probably only ten minutes. It couldn't have been easy for my friends to confront me, and it was even harder sitting humbly on the other side. But in that moment their yes to the Holy Spirit was the yes that changed the course and direction of my life.

Authentic and genuine friendships that hold us accountable to live a gospel-centered life are a true blessing. Related to that, hospitality is not just about setting the table but about creating a community of believers whose meaningful conversations bring glory to God and true-life change.

Those girls sat around me as my sisters in Christ, graciously rebuked my behavior and decisions, and called me to live a higher purpose. I knew they were right and changes had to be made. I had been convicted for weeks, if not months, that I was not living a life glorifying God, and I definitely wasn't expanding the kingdom. However, I had been choosing comfort and convenience over chasing him.

I'm unsure what my life would be like if those friends hadn't come around me and encouraged me to live a higher calling. I took that as a wake-up call to begin chasing harder after God. What I love about college is that when you leave campus for the summer, you can have a bit of a reset before you go back in the fall, and that was precisely what I did.

I spent the summer of 2010 chasing after Jesus, and when I came back for my senior year of college, I was more on fire for Jesus than I had been the previous three years.

My friends didn't have a table that we sat around to have that life-changing conversation; they didn't make a three-course meal. In fact, the closest thing we got to a meal in a dorm room was most likely popcorn and chocolate candies—a true nostalgic treat! But even though their hospitality wasn't constructed like the Pinterest-perfect, boho-themed dinner party our culture pressures us to have, it was authentic and centered around both obedience to God and welcoming me into a life of purpose and meaning.

That night my friends showed me what it looks like to love others well—outside your comfort zone and inside the will of God. The conversations, tears, and prayers showed me that even in the chaos, as uncomfortable as it might be, we can change lives with hospitality.

Encouragement Matters

If you are anything like me, hospitality is not natural, and you don't look for ways to invite people over. Yes, I've gotten better at it, because I've had to practice it over and over until it became second nature. It's a discipline that I've incorporated into my life.

One of the ways I practiced was by inviting people over and changing my focus. Instead of my focus being on the food or the decorations, I focused on how I could best encourage the people God had divinely placed at my table.

When I lived in South Carolina, one of my friends would ask, "Are you mad, sad, or glad?" She liked this question because it made us slow down and really consider how we were feeling. Since those specific words push us past surface-level emotions, we couldn't just give a quick or distracted answer, we had to be honest with our response. I loved this because when she asked me this question, she was intentional in listening to me and in her response. By asking this question when she hosted, my friend was also helping her guests open up and be semi-vulnerable about the state of their spirit.

I have enjoyed using this strategy as well. Sometimes not everyone around my table knows each other, so I have adapted it a bit. Next to my front door I place notecards and a pen so that guests can anonymously answer the question without feeling called out or intimidated around people they might not yet know. Once we start eating, I pull out the cards and pray for each one individually, creating a moment for encouragement and reflection in a setting where all are accepted as they are.

When I first started doing this, I was shocked at how many people would write about how they were mad or sad. Over time I've realized that people's lives weren't unusually bad or challenging. It was just that so many of them craved authentic connection. They needed a safe place to lay down their burdens and to be met with intentionality and encouragement just as they were, without expectation or pressure to change. When we invite people to the table, we're given an opportunity to create a warm space where everyone can feel seen and understood. It's a chance to be each other's cheerleaders and to build connections that feed our souls more deeply than words ever could.

In the Gospels we jump straight from Jesus' adolescence into his adult life, and one of the first things we see him do is build his community. He went out and found the tribe of men who would walk alongside him for the next few years. But what I think is more fascinating than Jesus building his community is how he did it. Those twelve disciples were fishermen, tax collectors, politicians, bookkeepers, and the list goes on. I believe God included the job titles of the disciples in Scripture to encourage us that they weren't all the same. Jesus was teaching us that we all belong here. No matter who you are—your background, where you come from, or who you are friends with—you belong.

How encouraging is it to be reminded by the God of the universe that you possess a specific purpose? How do you think those men felt when Jesus hand selected them? Aside from the fact that it was a strange man telling them to follow him, I'm sure they felt some affirmation or joy.

When building our tribe, when inviting people in, encouragement is an important ingredient we can't forget. In its simplest form, encouragement can be felt through words of affirmation that comfort us and others, meeting a deep human need that has been present since the beginning of time. Scripture reveals this desire clearly: Joshua was encouraged to "be strong and courageous. . . . for the Lord your God will be with you" (Josh. 1:9). In a time of distress, David "found strength in the Lord his God" (1 Sam. 30:6). And in the midst of uncontrollable circumstances, Daniel sought this affirmation from the Lord in the lion's den, and "no wound was found on him, because he had trusted in his God" (Dan. 6:23).

The true essence of encouragement lies in strengthening our hope and confidence in Jesus. By doing so, we can cultivate a more profound sense of trust and faith in his divine plan for our lives. Through encouragement we find the strength and resilience to overcome challenges and obstacles encountered along the way.

Take a moment to reflect on your life and contemplate the instances where a simple word of encouragement has ignited your faith, provided solace during moments of uncertainty, or empowered you to recognize your true potential and deepen your connection with God.

When Paul was building the church in Thessalonica, he gave them three different explicit charges to encourage each other: "Encourage one another with these words. . . . Encourage one another and build each other up. . . . We urge you, brothers and sisters . . . encourage the disheartened, help the weak, be patient with everyone" (1 Thess. 4:18; 5:11, 14).

Why did Paul focus on encouragement? When we try to live without confidence in Christ, we'll surely perish. That's what was happening in Thessalonica. The new church was trying to build up and grow in numbers despite persecution. Paul knew the only way to stay the course, to maintain the faith, and to have courage was to be encouraged by other believers.

However, Paul wasn't reassuring the church that they would be okay or that everything would work out. Biblical encouragement is the strengthening of faith. It means relying on God no matter the circumstances and knowing you have a tribe around you, lifting you up and spurring you on.

I love that term—*spurring*. I grew up in Arkansas, and I used to love watching the Canadian geese flying south every fall. Since we have a lot of lakes and ponds in Arkansas, it's a great place for the geese to land on their way to the bays and marshes of Louisiana and south Texas for the winter. When you watch geese fly, you notice they fly in a V formation. There are a lot of cool facts about the V formation, but my favorite is that it helps geese communicate. While flying, the goose at the point of the V faces the wind and creates air currents that help the other birds glide more easily. The others support and encourage that leader as they all fight against the strong wind. There is always a leader of the flock, but that leader doesn't stay in front for long. Soon another goose takes over, providing relief for the first. That's what our community should look like. We should be flying with our friends, moving in the same direction, spurring one another on in our flight. How does that look in your life? Are you encouraging your people?

Encouragement is about the life-giving power of living out the gospel, and one way we can do that is to cultivate the spiritual discipline of hospitality through the intentionality of the invitation.

Intentionality Matters

The true essence of hospitality lies in demonstrating love toward others by uplifting them with words of encouragement and intentionally inviting them in, saying, "You belong *here*." It's about creating a warm, welcoming atmosphere that makes people feel valued and loved.

Jesus did this throughout his ministry. He was constantly showing hospitality to others, and he didn't have a kitchen, a home, or even a table—but he found them! Let's look at one of the most famous stories of his ministry, the feeding of the five thousand.

> As evening approached, the disciples came to [Jesus] and said, "This is a remote place, and it's already getting late. Send the crowds away, so they can go to the villages and buy themselves some food."
>
> Jesus replied, "They do not need to go away. You give them something to eat."
>
> "We have here only five loaves of bread and two fish," they answered.
>
> "Bring them here to me," he said. And he directed the people to sit down on the grass. Taking the five loaves and the two fish and looking up to heaven, he gave thanks and broke the loaves. Then he gave them to the disciples, and the disciples gave them to the people. They all ate and were satisfied, and the disciples picked up twelve basketfuls of broken pieces that were left over. The number of those who ate was about five thousand men, besides women and children. (Matt. 14:15–21)

On a deserted hillside near the Sea of Galilee, a massive crowd had gathered to see Jesus. He felt for them, as they were hungry and spiritually thirsty. Even though they couldn't all sit around a table with him, he decided to do something incredible. Jesus fed not only their stomachs but also their souls with his act of profound kindness. Imagine how incredible it would have been to witness Jesus' extraordinary care, kindness, and intentionality.

The disciples responded like I probably would have,

practical and logical, suggesting that Jesus just move on and questioning how he was actually going to feed that large of a crowd. Yet Jesus saw beyond the physical hunger and lack of food or table. He recognized a deeper yearning, a thirst for connection, belonging, and the spiritual food he alone could offer. In his response lies the epitome of his intentionality: "They do not need to go away. You give them something to eat." Jesus didn't merely address the five thousand people's immediate need—hunger. He chose to involve the disciples; he chose to bring them along for the ride so that everyone could experience both a miracle and holy community.

In Jesus' hands the small basket of fish and loaves overflowed with abundance. It wasn't just a magical multiplication; it was a transformative one. He took what the people brought and the disciples presented and, with his divine power, provided for his people. He broke the bread, a symbolic gesture of giving, and with the disciples' help, he served the thousands.

Sharing food brings people together and creates a sense of community. Sharing a meal with others is a delightful experience that goes beyond filling our stomachs. It is an opportunity to connect with people on a deeper level—to share stories, laughter, and love. When we gather around a table, we nourish not only our bodies but also our souls. The joy of breaking bread together creates a sense of community and strengthens relationships. It is a beautiful reminder that food is not just fuel but a means to celebrate life and the people who make it worth living.

The feeding of the five thousand is more than a mere biblical event; it is a timeless message. It reminds us that

Let the Biscuits Burn

God's abundance is not limited by our perceived scarcity. Jesus' reaction to the disciples' skepticism encourages us to be intentional in our interactions, to see beyond the people and the resources that are right in front of us, and to be obedient in God's calling to love and serve others. Even when we cannot gather around a literal table, countless opportunities exist to create moments of connection, to nourish both body and soul, and to experience the abundance that flows from acts of love and generosity. Jesus recognized this on the hillside that day.

Think about the people in front of you. Imagine stepping outside your usual circles and looking with God's eyes at those in the periphery of your life. Beyond your close friends and your family, who has God placed within your reach? They might not be close confidantes or the people you spend loads of time with, but what if God is allowing you to cross paths with them for a meaningful and intentional purpose? They're your coworkers, neighbors, community members, and maybe even the stranger you've seen in the grocery store five times in the last month. God calls us to extend hospitality not only to those we naturally love but to anyone who may need to feel a sense of belonging.

This isn't about elaborate gestures or miraculous multiplication like with the loaves and fish. It's about recognizing the opportunities for connection in everyday moments. It's about offering a listening ear, a helping hand, and a kind word. It's about sharing our gifts, talents, and resources, no matter how limited they may seem. Just as Jesus multiplied five loaves and two fish to meet the needs of many, our small efforts can create ripples of encouragement, transforming our communities with care. Jesus modeled this by being fully present for those around him.

Reflecting on this example that Jesus gave us with the loaves and fish, ask yourself, *What does it mean to be truly present for someone, even when you can't physically be with them? How can I cultivate deep connection and support with others, even when separated by distance or circumstances?*

These questions challenge us to recognize that hospitality is as much about presence and prayer, as it is about proximity. By reimagining hospitality in this way, we can see each day's encounters as opportunities to nurture deeper connections and offer a sense of Christ's love to those around us.

We're in This Together

Community is not about perfection; it's about people. Jesus didn't invite the twelve disciples to a massive party to show off his home or try to win them over by buying them lavish gifts. He did bring five thousand of his closest friends to a perfectly constructed farmhouse table. He appealed to the inmost reality of people, ensuring that they felt seen. So when we are sitting around our table—whether it's the dining room table, the coffee table, or maybe a table at a local restaurant—we can show up for our people and increase their faith through the rhythm of hospitality. We can show those sitting across from us that we see them by listening to what's on their hearts and sharing how God has shown up for us during our own storms, revisiting his providence and sitting in his miracles.

When Jesus sought out the Twelve, he didn't require a certain social status or education level. He showed them divine hospitality by asking them to come hang out. Imagine how you would feel today if someone said, "Hey, I'd love to hang out with you. Want to grab some coffee this weekend?" You would most likely be affirmed and excited that someone desired to meet with you. It's encouraging to know you have been selected.

The best part is that we serve a God that came to earth to show us how to be hospitable and invite people in; he came to earth, embodied a human, and gave us tangible experiences to learn from. Just like it says in Hebrews 10:24–25, "Let us think of ways to motivate one another to acts of love and good works. And let us not neglect our meeting together, as some people do, but encourage one another, especially now that the day of his return is drawing near" (NLT).

Or as The Passion Translation interprets this passage: "Discover creative ways to encourage others and to motivate them toward acts of compassion, doing beautiful works as expressions of love. This is not the time to pull away and neglect meeting together, as some have formed the habit of doing. In fact, we should come together even more frequently, eager to encourage and urge each other onward as we anticipate that day dawning."[†]

[†] I wouldn't recommend using The Passion Translation as your main source, but it's an excellent translation for support and context.

True community can be found in pursuing this hope-filled, kingdom-focused hospitality day in and day out, not neglecting the discipline of serving others because we aren't sure we are good enough. Serving others doesn't focus on the perfection of people but dwells on seeing them as created in the image of God.

Hospitality isn't just for those who feel naturally gifted at it; it's a powerful way to encourage and uplift others. While Jesus walked the earth, he set the perfect example that hospitality should be the tone of our lives—how we approach relationships, work, conversations, and build our community. The Holy Spirit, the great encourager, works through our hospitality to create spaces where people feel seen, valued, and loved. When we open our hearts and homes, we create space to experience the Spirit's presence, recognize his movement in our lives, and share that encouragement with others.

We should be completely focused on the door—so intent on offering encouragement and uplifting those who arrive that we don't even hear the timer telling us the biscuits are done. Let the door captivate us. Let the arrival of others shift our attention away from the distractions the Enemy tries to use. And let's allow the biscuits to burn while we wholeheartedly invest in loving and encouraging people.

Part 1
The Preparation

Chapter 2
Unpacking Hospitality

There it sits—the elephant in the living room—draped in linen tablecloths and adorned with perfectly polished silverware. It looms large in our minds, casting a shadow of inadequacy: hospitality. This word often leaves a bad taste in our mouths, initiating avoidance because we are insecure about our abilities. It's most likely a word you've heard ad nauseam. You can't even define it, let alone emulate it. In our culture *hospitality* can be an overspiritualized and intimidating word, conjuring images of perfection that are all but impossible to achieve, a benchmark with failure written all over it. We scroll through picture-perfect Instagram feeds, browse curated Pinterest boards, and sigh, defeated, as Martha Stewart whispers in our ears, "Your home? Not

The Preparation

quite magazine worthy." But here's the thing: What you're thinking about isn't hospitality; it's entertaining.

Martha Stewart wrote in her book *Entertaining*, "Entertaining, like cooking, is a little selfish, because it really involves pleasing yourself with a guest list that will coalesce into your ideal of harmony, with a menu orchestrated to your home and taste, with decorations subject to your own eye. Given these considerations, it has to be pleasureful."[1] There you go. In that one quote Martha helps us understand the heart behind entertaining. It serves self. It is focused on the look-at-me factor, ensuring that everyone who enters acknowledges the host and the environment. It places presentation over people. The heart behind the invite isn't to make outsiders feel like insiders; the heart behind the invite is about elevating the host's appearance.

Hospitality takes a different approach.

Rather than inviting the guest inside and showing off everything from the décor to the food, biblical hospitality aims to welcome all with a greeting that makes the invited feel like royalty showing up to a feast. Just as Jesus invites us to be the VIP guest at the table, we, too, should treat everyone we invite with the same splendor and attention. I love how Matt Chandler defines biblical hospitality: "To give loving welcome to those outside your normal circle of friends. It's opening your life and your house to those who believe differently than you do." He then encourages us by saying, "Welcome everyone you meet."[2]

Hospitality goes beyond the quality of the food, the trendiness of the décor, or the brilliance of the conversation. It's about having a heart for Christ and demonstrating

Unpacking Hospitality

his love by coming alongside others to meet their needs. When we start to see hospitality in this way, we will discover countless opportunities to serve and find joy in serving others. Our primary motivation for inviting people into our homes should be to help them grow closer to Jesus. Hospitality should be a means of demonstrating how good Christ is, regardless of what amenities we might offer.

I find there can be a bit of confusion around the terms *hospitality* and *entertaining* because they are used interchangeably in most circles. In an effort to provide clarity and ensure that we are moving in the same direction, I've created a table to help you better understand how they are different.

ENTERTAINING	HOSPITALITY
Always having everything perfectly hot and ready at the same time.	Sometimes burning the next course, because you were so wrapped up in loving the people at your table.
Spending the entire week leading up to the party dusting baseboards and replacing tattered throw pillows.	Inviting people into your space authentically, no matter the size, the mess, or the decade-old décor.
Makes everything about perfection.	Makes everything about people.

The Preparation

While both of these terms involve welcoming people into our homes, their underlying motivations and focus differ significantly. Entertaining often centers around creating a polished experience, prioritizing the environment, and making sure everything looks and feels a certain way. Entertaining often takes a lot of time to plan exactly what the experience will be like for your guests. In contrast, hospitality is rooted in genuine care for others, offering a warm and welcoming space that enables guests to feel safe and secure. It's forgetting self and prioritizing whoever walks through the door. To determine whether your approach leans toward entertaining or hospitality, ask yourself these questions:

- *Is my primary goal to impress guests with a flawlessly executed event or to genuinely connect with and care for them?*
- *Do I spend excessive energy on surface-level details or prioritize creating a comfortable and inviting atmosphere?*
- *Do I deviate from my original vision to meet the needs of my guests or rigidly adhere to a predetermined schedule?*
- *Do I present a curated version of myself or share my true self with my guests, imperfections and all?*

By reflecting on these questions, you can gain a clearer understanding of your motivations and strive to cultivate a spirit of hospitality.

When you welcome someone into your home with sincere hospitality, they're not inspecting your living space for dust bunnies or evaluating your housekeeping skills based on the number of dishes in the sink. Instead, they're seeking connection and a feeling of being cared for. So the next time you're hesitant to invite people in, remember that the most important thing you can do is focus on them and help them feel welcome and valued.

We open our doors not because we are serving self but because we are loving Christ. Hospitality is about creating an atmosphere of love, warmth, and acceptance. It is about creating a space where people feel seen, heard, and valued. It's about opening our hearts and our homes to others, just as Christ has opened his heart to us.

Hospitality isn't about replicating magazine spreads or Pinterest perfection. It's not about being Joanna Gaines with a magazine-worthy home and the smell of freshly baked sourdough permeating the kitchen. It's not even about having a gift. No, hospitality is far more relational, far more accessible, and infinitely more transformative.

What the Bible Says About Hospitality

As women, we can feel the pressure to be perfect in every aspect of our lives. From our appearance to our home décor, we strive for a level of excellence that is often exhausting. When it comes to hospitality, this pressure can be overwhelming. As we embark on this journey, we must first acknowledge where we sit with this concept of hospitality. Have you been hiding behind deceptive thoughts like, *But I'm just not good at hosting?* Are you nervous and unsure of

The Preparation

the invitation God is calling you to extend to your neighbors, or have you picked up this book as a way to brush up on your skills and take the next step in your hospitality journey?

Don't worry. I'd say we're all a little nervous. And we can all agree that there is room for learning about and growing in hospitality. But by the grace of Jesus we are able to pursue characteristics that draw us closer to the heart of God. And that is what practicing hospitality does; it draws us closer to God, to Christlikeness.

What if your heart wasn't focused on creating the perfect environment for entertaining but on making your home purposeful for the kingdom? What if instead of elevating yourself above the broken world outside, you invited that world inside?

Hospitality is not just a nice thing to do; it's a biblical command. In Romans 12:13 we're told to "share with the Lord's people who are in need. Practice hospitality." In Hebrews 13:2 we are reminded to "show hospitality to strangers, for by so doing some people have shown hospitality to angels without knowing it." In the Bible we see countless examples of hospitality: Abraham welcomed three strangers into his home and provided them with food and shelter (Gen. 18:1–8). The Shunammite woman provided a room for the prophet Elisha whenever he passed through her town (2 Kings 4:8–11). In the New Testament the Gospels show Jesus having meals with and showing hospitality to others during his ministry on earth. Even after his resurrection Jesus provided fish and bread for his disciples after a long night of fishing (John 21:1–14).

Let's just call a spade a spade: I think that Jesus' love language was food, because—I mean—he loved eating with people. Our King is seeking to make himself more known through our obedience of loving others at the table. And I'm confident our lives will be changed by the intimacy we experience when extending the invite becomes second nature, when we can open our doors and fill our tables, and when we get to the place where this radical love becomes our habit.

Hospitality Is About Opening Your Heart

Most of us weren't destined to write cookbooks or host lavish parties. But we were all created for community. Genesis 1:1 starts Scripture off strong by showing us that God loves community. The Trinity reveals to us that God, in his inmost reality, is a communal God. If he desired that within himself, why would he not then desire that for his children? I am convinced that hospitality is one of the most important spiritual disciplines we can cultivate because it leads to connection and community. We cannot sit idle on the sidelines of our lives waiting for the perfect house or family or moment to be hospitable with. In our fast-paced, tech-saturated, give-it-to-me-now culture, we need to rediscover the blessing of a slow meal around a table with people we care about. Then we can build our community and draw people in.

Hospitality is about vulnerability. It's about sharing our lives, flaws and all, with another human being. It's about

The Preparation

stepping out of our comfort zones, extending a hand of grace, and saying, "Come, sit with me. Be seen. Be heard. Be welcomed."

Think of Mary and Martha, that iconic duo from Bethany.

> As Jesus and his disciples were on their way, he came to a village where a woman named Martha opened her home to him. She had a sister called Mary, who sat at the Lord's feet listening to what he said. But Martha was distracted by all the preparations that had to be made. She came to him and asked, "Lord, don't you care that my sister has left me to do the work by myself? Tell her to help me!"
>
> "Martha, Martha," the Lord answered, "you are worried and upset about many things, but few things are needed—or indeed only one. Mary has chosen what is better, and it will not be taken away from her." (Luke 10:38–42)

Martha bustled about, her apron a badge of domestic expertise. Mary sat at Jesus' feet, soaking in his words, unmoved by the chaos. While Martha fretted and fumed, Mary embodied hospitality—not in the outward flurry of activity but in the inward posture of intentionality.

And Jesus? He doesn't chastise Martha for her Martha-ness or demand Pinterest-worthy platters and spotless floors. He simply affirms Mary's choice—the choice to prioritize communion.

You see, hospitality isn't about performance. It's about

connection. It's about creating a space where love takes center stage. It's about offering a refuge, a breath of fresh air, a slice of your life shared with another.

Hospitality is often considered to be the embodiment of love, as it's the foundation from which all other expressions of love flow. In fact, some argue that it's the very essence of demonstrating love.[3] When we view love as the center of a wheel, hospitality becomes the crucial conduit through which all other spokes of love are conveyed. Whether it takes the form of intentionality, friendship, service, or any other manifestation of love, hospitality is a necessary component for these traits to be effectively demonstrated.

The beauty lies in the unexpected. The divine resides in the cups of tea forgotten and cold, the laughter that masks the burnt dinner, and the heartfelt conversation that transcends the chipped china. It's in the messy, unscripted moments and the genuine smiles exchanged over mismatched plates that the heart of hospitality is shown. This is when lives can be changed.

Don't get me wrong; I love a table set for a five-course meal as much as the queen of England, and God shows up there too. But something uniquely intimate happens when we strip away the pomp and circumstance. When we offer our homes and our spaces just as they are, we create moments for vulnerable and authentic conversation.

Those conversations usually happen when dirty dishes are in the sink. Why do dirty dishes matter? I have no clue. My only guess is that when dishes are in my sink, it creates a subconscious connection that we are all a mess. There is camaraderie being in the trenches of life together. The

The Preparation

coolest part is that Jesus shows up to those trenches of life's conversations and moves. You can feel his presence just as if he were sitting around the table communing with us.

I will never back down from inviting people into my home, no matter the state of my house or apartment, the dirty dishes in the sink, or the dust collecting around the baseboards. I've learned that as long as I supply a place to eat dinner, God will facilitate the rest.

● ● ● ● ● ●

Over watercooler talk one day, between racing from one meeting to the other, I invited several of my single friends from work over for Galentine's dinner. We delegated drinks and desserts and planned to see each other later. The plan was to meet after work around six, which gave me approximately forty-five minutes to get home, see what in the world I was going to cook, and make my apartment seem somewhat welcoming. I made it home in time to make a one-pot kitchen-sink chicken dish that I recall sharing the recipe for, because the girls just loved it so much. Don't ask me specifics now, because I most likely just threw stuff together!

The conversation was lively; we laughed, prayed, and cried. It was vulnerable, real, and authentic. The night lasted well past my bedtime, and when all was said and done, one of the girls hugged my neck on her way out and said, "This was exactly what I needed. Your God is using you in big ways." And then she made a silly joke about my laundry being in piles on the floor.

I responded by laughing about my laundry with a

side-eye roll and then quickly chimed in, "My God sees you and knows what you are going through. My door is always open."

I knew this friend wasn't a believer. If I could build relationships with people at work and help them feel comfortable enough to come over for a meal, God would show up and begin to work a change in their hearts. All God needed was my yes. That night wasn't the first time she came into my home, and it wasn't the last. My spontaneous invite at work turned into a friendship, and on many Saturday mornings I'd wake up to a text asking if I could put cinnamon rolls in the oven and she'd bring the coffee.

Authentic relationship-building happens in the unplanned, unscripted moments of hospitality, when we put aside our self-centered motives and approach our yes with a posture of obedience.

Chapter 3

• • • • •

The Spiritual Discipline of Hospitality

To approach this book with a receptive posture, understanding the definition of *hospitality* is important. Maybe even more important is understanding that hospitality, while a spiritual gift that some are given by the Holy Spirit, is also a spiritual discipline. But before we can understand hospitality as a spiritual discipline, we need to understand what a spiritual discipline is. Here's how I would define it: a spiritual growth practice in which we draw closer to God's character by cultivating habits and rhythms that glorify him.

Spiritual disciplines help us experientially put into practice what the Holy Spirit is teaching us through Scripture

The Preparation

and discernment. Like any discipline, it requires restraint, practice, focus, and responsibility. And unlike spiritual gifts, everyone has the ability to discipline themselves around practices that help us mature in our faith.

Spiritual disciplines can include studying the Bible, meditating on and memorizing God's Word, fasting, and worship. Theologians much smarter than me divide these disciplines into categories. We'll keep things somewhat elementary when it comes to spiritual disciplines, focusing on cultivating a posture of obedience. Unless you're writing a thesis on the subject, we can skip the deeper theological categories, which can get pretty heady.

William James, a philosopher and the father of American psychology, once noted, "Habit is a second nature." Yet, in a world saturated with distractions and instant gratification, it has become increasingly difficult to cultivate positive habits and break free from negative ones. We live in a culture that promotes and encourages addictive habits and behaviors that draw us into distraction and away from real life, avoiding meaningful connections and experiences.

Habits shape how we live, often without us even noticing. As James pointed out, habits become second nature, guiding our actions. To truly live in obedience to God, we need to be intentional about building habits that help us grow closer to God to experience him more intimately. Spiritual disciplines are the practices that keep us focused on God and who he is; they help us fight against distractions and stay grounded in our faith. This kind of discipline is exactly what Paul encouraged—staying persistent and eager in doing good. When we make these habits part of our lives, we create space to grow closer to God and reflect his character.

Overall, our society is on a steep decline in living a disciplined life. Paul wrote in Romans 12:11, "Never be lazy, but work hard and serve the Lord enthusiastically" (NLT). And to the church in Galatia, Paul encouraged, "Let's not get tired of doing what is good. At just the right time we will reap a harvest of blessing if we don't give up" (Gal. 6:9 NLT). If we truly want to live a life marked by glorifying God in all we do, we must fight against the cultural pressures of laziness and the idolatry of self and begin to draw closer to Christ through living a disciplined life. We do that by cultivating spiritual disciplines that produce good fruit and drench our souls in his character.

Focus and Sacrifice

As we think about discipline, I'm sure there are a few areas in your life that immediately come to mind. For me it's my diet. Mostly because—well, let's just say I have a very committed relationship with carbs. Discipline in that area is not exactly my strong suit.

Now my sister? She's the kind of person who makes discipline look easy. She's consistent in how she eats, moves her body, prays, stays connected to friends, reads meaningful books, and keeps up with her hobbies. Honestly, if there were Olympic medals for being disciplined, she'd have a few golds.

A perfect example of this came out during our pageant

The Preparation

days. Neither of us grew up doing pageants, but when I got to college, I set my sights on the Miss Arkansas crown. I gave it a solid four-year run of glitz, grit, and almosts. I didn't win, and after the fourth try I decided to hang up my heels.

Enter my sister. I like to think she was inspired by my valiant attempts (and maybe some leftover spray tan). I was genuinely over-the-moon proud when she took home the coveted title of Miss Arkansas's Outstanding Teen—and okay, maybe just a tiny bit salty. Not because she didn't deserve it but because it felt like I put in the same amount of effort and came up short.

Have you ever been there? Watching something come so easily for someone else, while your own journey feels like a never-ending uphill climb?

I remember wrestling with that. I had put in effort, right? Then I talked to a wise woman at church, Mrs. Trish, who kindly reminded me that discipline isn't about occasional bursts of motivation. It's about the long game. Consistent, steady, often unglamorous effort.

Looking back it's easy to see the difference between my sister and me. My sister didn't just prepare for the pageant season. She lived with discipline year-round. Whether it was dancing in the studio or reading at home, she kept showing up. Me? I procrastinated. I'd hit the gas pedal only when the pageant was near, leading to last-minute cram sessions, forgotten lyrics, and crash workouts to try to catch up on the months I'd taken off.

Here's the truth: My sister's consistency paid off in scholarship money, confidence, and endurance, while my approach led to a great story and some tears. And what I learned—and continue to learn to this day—is that to grow, we must be disciplined, and that takes consistent focus and sacrifice.

Discipline doesn't have to come naturally to be powerful. It just has to come consistently. And if you, like me, aren't naturally wired for structure, take heart. We don't need to be great at it. We just need to start and show up.

Cultivating the Discipline of Hospitality

I don't know about you, but when I hear the word *discipline* I immediately think of my alarm going off before I'm ready or trying to resist that tempting dessert at night. Discipline can feel overwhelming and hard to keep up with, but spiritual disciplines aren't meant to be stressful or difficult to achieve. In fact, when we approach them with the right mindset, they become life-giving habits that deepen our relationship with God. The goal is to create space for him to shape us and transform our hearts with a Christlike love that puts his glory on display.

Spiritual disciplines might push us out of our comfort zone and work muscles we're not used to, but that's only because they haven't become second nature yet. If you read this book with the mindset of dredging through mud, hospitality will be hard. But if you read this book with a growth mindset, praying for your heart to change and for you to grow deeper in community with God and his people, you will finish equipped to open your door and

The Preparation

invite others in. The spiritual disciplines are for our growth and for our blessing. They are instruments that help us grow closer to God and experience his goodness and his character in new ways.

John Mark Comer, in a podcast with Annie F. Downs, said it like this: "Spiritual disciplines are a . . . tool that's a part of this larger kind of human growth idea of spiritual formation. Spiritual formation is the process by which we are formed into people of Christlike love, yes, through deepening surrender to—in union with the Father and the Son and the Spirit."[1]

We should always remember that the whole point of any spiritual discipline is to love God and live for him. It's not legalistic or about checking the box. It's about drawing closer to our Creator and understanding more of who he is. Practicing the spiritual discipline of hospitality won't change your life overnight, and perhaps you won't be good at it for a while, but I guarantee that with every single door you open and every seat at the table you fill, your heart will be changed.

When we look at hospitality not as just a gift but as a spiritual discipline, we are held accountable for directing our attention, efforts, and resources toward cultivating a life that exemplifies God and his nature. We focus on developing the skills needed to make hospitality second nature and viewing our insecurities as the Enemy's breeding ground. We turn our maybes into yeses, and our obedience begins to manifest itself into divine moments around our tables with neighbors who become friends and friends who become family.

The Spiritual Discipline of Hospitality
How to Form a Habit of Hospitality

I'm not a morning bird; I'm a night owl. I love staying up late, and I can welcome the sun with the best of them. But I learned that while I was staying up late, I was filling my mind and body with not-great things. I would routinely binge-watch reality TV shows until well into the early morning hours and eat snacks only teenage boys should eat. I'd wake up in the morning—after hitting the Snooze button twelve times—with the best intentions to spend my evening in quiet solace with the Lord. But seven or eight o'clock would roll around, and I'd find myself camped out in the same spot as the previous evening, watching these TV shows that did nothing but steal my joy through comparison.

For myriad reasons I decided to make a change. Ultimately, I read that successful people wake up early and start their day slowly, and their first habit? Making their bed. So I began that habit of waking up slowly, making my bed, and then spending time with God.

It was not easy the first few mornings, but over time, with consistency and a lot of Snooze buttons, I created a habit that changed the trajectory of my entire day. The rhythm of waking up early provided the space I needed to have quiet time with the Lord. Because I followed the slow rhythm of waking up, getting ready, and preparing mentally for what the day could bring, I was no longer stressed, running late, cranky, or short-tempered. I was thoughtful and relaxed, and I found that the way I was treating others was directly correlated with my mornings. My productivity skyrocketed, and I was able to be intentional with how I showed God's grace

The Preparation

and love to my coworkers. I also found that waking up early required me to go to bed earlier, so I didn't have time for television to permeate my mind and consume my thoughts. I was now prioritizing true, right, honorable things (Phil. 4:8) and spending my time not with reality television but with Jesus.

Jeffrey Schwartz, a research psychologist at UCLA's School of Medicine, makes the case that spiritual growth can play a significant role in habit formation. By cultivating positive emotions, reducing stress, and increasing self-awareness, spiritual practices help create an environment more conducive for change. Additionally, spiritual beliefs can provide motivation and inspiration to persevere in the face of challenges.[2] Makes sense why starting my morning rhythm helped me show more grace toward myself and my coworkers.

When James Clear wrote *Atomic Habits*, he broke a habit-forming process into four categories: cue, craving, response, and reward. "The cue triggers a craving, which motivates a response, which provides a reward, which satisfies the craving and, ultimately, becomes associated with the cue. Together, these four steps form a neurological feedback loop—cue, craving, response, reward; cue, craving, response, reward—that ultimately allows you to create automatic habits."[3] While this process is great for creating habits like getting in the gym or eating better, when developing a spiritual discipline, it's not about our own strength or our own process. The habit formation of a spiritual discipline is about how we lean not on our own understanding (Prov. 3:5) and involve the Spirit.

Taking Clear's four-step approach as a springboard, I am proposing a four-step approach to habit forming that relies on the Spirit's discernment and direction. To cultivate the spiritual discipline of hospitality, we first need to set the rhythm in which we will practice it, which influences why we are doing it. Once we understand when and why we are doing it, we need to be obedient and trust the process, which ultimately leads to the habit being cultivated. Cultivating the habit of hospitality is basically creating a new system or process by which we view the world, but instead of viewing the world through a secular lens, we view the world through the eyes of God.

Let's dive a little deeper.

1. Set the Rhythm

Every habit we develop begins with a rhythm that we need to cultivate. When it comes to creating a good habit, we need to identify new rhythms that we can associate with the desired outcome. Define what that rhythm needs to be by identifying what might trigger you to act. Is there a specific time of day that triggers this rhythm or desired outcome?

As we begin to develop the habit of hospitality, we need to create a rhythm of inviting people in. By creating a set time every week or every month to invite people in, we will prepare our hearts and our minds not only to open our door and extend the welcome but also to allow the Spirit in to renew our souls. What does the rhythm look like for you? Fill in the blanks below:

I will invite _____
                name of person or group of people

over _____ a _____.
     once / twice / three times   week / month

The Preparation

2. Know Your Why

When creating a habit, you need to understand your why—the reason you are doing it. Galatians 5:16 says, "So I say, walk by the Spirit, and you will not gratify the desires of the flesh." When we walk by the Spirit and align our desires with the will and desires of God, the Spirit prompts our hearts to develop certain habits to draw us closer to him.

There are a few different reasons that we desire a habit of hospitality. For me, it became a rhythm I pursued because I desired a godly community. I was inspired by 1 Peter 4:8–9, which says, "Above all, love each other deeply, because love covers over a multitude of sins. Offer hospitality to one another without grumbling." That might be the same reason you pursue it. However, I think my reason is now slightly different after years of practicing this habit.

Today I would say the reason I pursue hospitality is to make heaven crowded. I want to bring people in and share the magnificent love of Christ with them. Maybe you've heard of the Great Commission. It comes from Matthew 28:18–20: "Then Jesus came to them and said, 'All authority in heaven and on earth has been given to me. Therefore go and make disciples of all nations, baptizing them in the name of the Father and of the Son and of the Holy Spirit, and teaching them to obey everything I have commanded you. And surely I am with you always, to the very end of the age.'"

Last, maybe the Spirit is trying to develop in you godly characteristics—"love, joy, peace, forbearance, kindness, goodness, faithfulness, gentleness and self-control" (Gal. 5:22–23)—and this discipline is drawing you closer to him.

Ask yourself, *Why is hospitality important to me? Why did I pick up this book?* Maybe you desperately want to be good at inviting people in. Maybe you've been practicing this rhythm for a while and you've become a Martha—laser-focused on the party and not the people—and you want to make a change, to infuse Jesus into the middle of the rhythm of hospitality in your life.

Whatever your why, write it down and say it out loud. The more you identify your reason, the more focused you'll be on why you want to make a change and the more motivated you'll be to trust the process.

3. Trust the Process

Now that you have set your rhythm and identified your why, you need to put it into practice. It's not quite a habit at this point; it's a practice that you are putting into place. When my son, John Maverick, was born, I quickly realized how challenging it was to establish any kind of routine. My days were filled with the unpredictability of feedings, diaper changings, and sleepless nights. At first the idea of forming habits felt impossible. But little by little I started setting small goals: a morning walk with my son, a quiet moment of prayer before bed, and even taking time to just sit and breathe in the stillness while he slept on me after nursing. It wasn't easy, and some days it felt like I was failing. But as the weeks went by, those small habits started to shape the rhythm of my days. The more consistent I became, the more natural it felt to build those moments of peace into my chaotic new-mom life. It took practice, patience, and grace—just like any habit worth forming.

The Preparation

The Spirit is beckoning you to slow down, dig in, and trust the process of building the rhythm of spiritual disciplines in your life. Listen to the small voice inside your soul and be consistent. Paul wrote in his letter to the Philippians that we can be confident that God began a good work in us and will carry it to completion until the day of Christ Jesus (Phil. 1:6). Now, Paul was speaking to the church in Philippi and praying that they continue to seek God, mature, and strengthen their relationships through the process of sanctification. We are, in a sense, walking through sanctification to become more like Jesus, like the Philippians. Just as Paul prayed that the church in Philippi would strengthen and mature in Christ until the end, we can be confident that by trusting the process and creating habits that draw us closer to Jesus, we will, in turn, strengthen and mature in him.

4. Cultivate the Habit

For us to become experts in hospitality and to rest in the habit we've formed, we must be consistent. The rhythm you set in step 1 was intended to keep you consistent and faithful to complete the good work, because Jesus wants to pour blessing after blessing on you for being obedient to your faith in him.

If we fail to be consistent or to allow the Spirit to transform our lives through cultivating habits, we won't produce the fruit that helps us reflect the goodness of who God is. Ultimately, that's our goal with habitual hospitality, right? That we would be a people who welcome without inhibition, reflect the kindness of a God who wants to sit with us, and open the door and help people enter a deeper and more intimate relationship with Jesus.

Habits are complicated, and how we cultivate them is influenced by how we were raised, our environment, our beliefs, and our education. Our behaviors directly affect the way our habits are formed. Luckily, we've all been welcomed in by God. We've all been included in the family of Christ. So let Hebrews encourage us: "Let us strip off every [excuse for not practicing habitual hospitality], especially the [excuses that keep us from experiencing God and his welcome] that so easily trip us up. And let us [practice hospitality] with endurance [in] the race that God has set before us" (12:1 NLT).

• • • • • •

When we finally reach a life marked by habitual hospitality, we find that it brings *us* life. If we allow habitual hospitality to be as second nature as breathing, if we allow it to be our way of life, we will reflect the welcome extended by our good and gracious Father. It's not about the perfection or the pomp and circumstance. It's about the people, the relationships, the kindness we showed, the love we extended, and the faith in a loving God we displayed.

Chapter 4

Preparing Your Heart

Every day, whether we realize it or not, we are constantly making preparations for what's ahead. My week starts with grocery shopping and meal planning. Each morning we prepare for the day by getting dressed. Throughout the day, no matter where we are, we're always preparing for what's to come.

As a new mother, one big lesson I've learned is that my entire day revolves around preparing my son, John Maverick, for bedtime. If he hasn't had enough to eat, a regular sleep routine, or stimulating play during the day, it means I haven't prepared well and my night will be filled with midnight feedings and moments of wakefulness. The entire framework of our lives emphasizes the importance of preparation, as it helps create rhythms that benefit us.

The Preparation

Sometimes creating these rhythms can be challenging, like adding more water to your diet or going to bed earlier so you can wake up to work out. By being intentional about our decisions, we can drastically change our lives one step at a time.

The Two-Top

After grad school I worked in college athletics and moved every year for several years. While it seemed fun and adventurous, it made building a community difficult. Just as I was getting comfortable—learning the neighborhood, making friends, and really liking where I was living—I'd have to move again. When I moved to Birmingham, Alabama, the change was significant, as I downsized from a spacious apartment to a modest one with limited space. The living area in my new apartment was quite small, and I had to let go of the huge table I'd had in my previous place. This large table was hardly used, so I didn't mind parting with it.

In my new apartment there wasn't much room for additional furniture, and I struggled to fit even a fridge and a stove. It felt smaller than any other place I'd lived in, almost like a suite at a cheap hotel. Despite feeling a bit lonely in my new city, I rarely invited people over and hardly cooked at home. My job in athletics at Samford University kept me busy, and most of my meals were either on campus or catered by vendors at the sporting events I worked. Having a table seemed like the least of my concerns at the time.

However, my mom felt that a table would make the

space feel more homey. So we found a small drop-leaf one at a local upcycle store in town and paid only ten dollars for it. I remember grumbling and complaining about setting up that small table because I thought I would never use it.

Looking back, I realize how much that small two-top table meant to me. It not only served its practical purpose, but it also held a deeper significance. If only I could go back and have a conversation with my twenty-five-year-old self about the importance of that table and the significance that Scripture places on centering our lives around the table.

God, in his infinite wisdom, knew exactly what he was doing.

He was preparing my heart to learn about his design for the table. Although my heart was not remotely ready to receive that divine wisdom, God had already put the wheels in motion. Over the next nine months that two-top table would change my life.

Out of all my transitions, the move to Birmingham was the toughest. For some reason finding community was especially hard, and as an outgoing person, not having weekend plans or friends to hang out with wasn't what I had imagined for this new chapter. I had been encouraged by my mom (after tearfully expressing how lonely I was) to lean into the one friend I had there, Katie, and be intentional about inviting her over for dinner. I really didn't understand why it was so important that I invite her over. My apartment was small, my table was embarrassing, and I didn't really know how to cook. Could we not just go out to dinner? My mom insisted

The Preparation

that there was something special about being obedient and inviting others to the table. She told me to pray about the dinner, prepare the food, and have an expectant heart for what God would do.

I took my mom's advice and invited Katie over for dinner, and I remember making this horrible cheese tortellini. Tortellini is easy. Pasta meet Sauce. Done. However, my prideful self decided to take the recipe into my own hands and add more cheese to the pasta instead of adding a sauce. The recipe didn't turn out great, but you know what did turn out great? The conversation.

That night was the start of something I never could have imagined. God took that small act of obedience in showing hospitality to Katie and, in a matter of weeks, turned it into a Bible study with between five and eight women in my small apartment enjoying the community built around his faithfulness. Those women experienced Christ as we walked through Scripture. We prayed over deep-seated faithlessness, and we renewed our commitment to following Jesus.

Not only did God reveal himself to those women in that season, but he blessed my obedience with a community of Christian women who filled my soul as much as I filled their stomachs. I had never experienced God that way. Yes, I had seen God provide before, but for him to fill my longing for community and friendship while putting his glory on display was so edifying. It reminded me that I serve a God who is bigger than a lonely Friday night or a table for one.

Tune Your Heart

Preparation isn't about how good the food tastes or what the table looks like; preparation is all about the heart. Our hearts must be so saturated in Christ that our lives, every rhythm and practice, glorify God. What does Scripture say about preparing our hearts?

- 2 Chronicles 12:14 warns us against disregarding preparation for our heart: "He did evil because he had not set his heart on seeking the Lord."
- Job 11:13 teaches us that through prayer, we should prepare our hearts: "If only you would prepare your heart and lift up your hands to him in prayer!" (NLT).
- Psalm 78:8 references the need for heart preparation: "And not be like their fathers, a stubborn and rebellious generation, a generation that did not prepare its heart and whose spirit was not faithful to God" (NASB).
- Proverbs 4:23 encourages us to prepare our hearts so we are fit for worship and ministry: "Guard your heart above all else, for it determines the course of your life" (NLT).
- James 1:25 says that those who prioritize the preparation of their hearts will be blessed in all they do: "Whoever looks intently into the perfect law that gives freedom, and continues in it—not forgetting what they have heard, but doing it—they will be blessed in what they do."

The Preparation

Preparing our hearts for a life focused on reflecting Christ through hospitality means that we walk into each day with our hands (and our doors) open to the Lord using us (and our tables) for his plan and purpose. If I hadn't been walking into that dinner with Katie with my hands open, ready for God to use me, I would have missed out on an immense blessing he desired to give me. God doesn't want to be an authoritarian forcing us to be obedient; he wants us to be prepared to walk in obedience so he can overflow his blessings upon us.

What is your heart focused on?

You may have come across the Instagram videos where the entire family runs through the house in chaos, attempting to leave in time for Sunday morning church. The chaos doesn't end there. The video then shows the kids arguing in the back seat while the parents in the front complain about various things. Finally, as the car pulls into the church parking lot and Dad parks, Mom yells, "Everyone stop arguing and smile." The video ends with the family happily skipping into church, seemingly ignoring the fact that they had been yelling just a few moments before.

This is exactly what Satan wants.

Now, yes, the video is funny. Oddly enough, we have probably all been there at some point. But is this what our hearts should be focused on? Is this what a prepared heart looks like as we enter God's house to worship him?

Worship is the posture we were created to live in. A. W. Tozer described worship like this: "Yes, worship of the loving God is man's whole reason for existence. That is why we are born, and that is why we are born again from above."[1]

We were designed by a Creator to fully and wholly reflect his goodness and glory to those around us. Worship is a mindset, and because we are carnal, selfish beings, it does not come naturally. We can be ready to worship when we walk out the door on Sunday morning but distracted and arguing two minutes later in the car. Worship requires focus and preparation.

Have you heard the saying "Prepare your hearts for worship"? One of my favorite hymns states it this way: "Tune my heart to sing Thy grace . . . Prone to wander, Lord, I feel it."[2]

Does that ring true in your own life? Because it does in mine. In that one lyric I've found both the problem and the need for spiritual preparation.

My heart wanders.

I'm constantly comparing my home, my table, my food, my invitation. Here is where I fall short. I'm not comparing myself to the standards outlined in Scripture. I am comparing myself to the world's standards. Standards that have been forced in my face through social media and what our culture deems as quintessentially hospitable.

Just like a piano's music goes flat and off-key when untuned or athletes lose their edge when they don't train, our hearts will wander if we don't consistently focus and tune them back to the truths of Scripture.

What does the tuning process look like for our hearts? It's in the daily rhythms and practices we align ourselves with. The Enemy desires the dissonance and discord that comes from being out of tune. Satan wants nothing more than for us to be sitting in the passenger seat of the car,

The Preparation

headed to church in chaos and ignoring the fact that we are entering a place to worship the Most High God.

• • • • • •

I didn't invite Katie over on a whim; I'd been wrestling with my loneliness and longing for community for months. Throughout that time I prayed earnestly, sought wise counsel, and immersed myself in Scripture, patiently waiting for the Lord to guide my steps and provide as Jehovah Jireh. I was obediently waiting (*impatiently* could probably also be used here; surely I'm not the only one!), sitting with Scripture daily and longing to hear from him.

Here is my shameless plug for quiet journaling time. Sometimes journaling feels monotonous and overwhelming. It's slow and my thoughts are fast and what do I even write? But I've found that journaling is a way I can reflect on what God has done in my life. I can look back and see how he used my table in a lonely season and provided for me, because I journaled about the struggle, the provision, and his faithfulness. Don't sleep on journaling; it'll change your life and your perspective.

My journey wasn't perfect. Many days my journal entries resembled the musings of a frustrated child not getting her way, and my prayers often sounded more like a toddler's temper tantrum. Yet, in my human imperfections, the Lord understood my heart—and he understands yours too. He doesn't seek perfection; he seeks our obedience.

Tuning our hearts to allow God to use us takes effort. It's in preparation that we begin to see people the way God sees them, and we start to experience God in a new way through hospitality. Elijah didn't hear God speak the first time he sought him in the wilderness in Beersheba. Elijah was looking for God in the wind, the earthquake, and the fire, but, instead, God used a small voice (1 Kings 19:11–13). Elijah's experience in seeking God reminds us that God is ever faithful and will always prepare us to fulfill his will.

Hospitality isn't something that just unfolds spontaneously in the chaos of life; it grows from a heart prepared and focused on serving others. That's how we tune our hearts to Jesus, by spending time with him and letting his presence shape and prepare us. When we're grounded in him, we can step out in obedience, inviting others to experience his love around our table, even if the biscuits are burned and the house is a mess. What truly matters is the posture of our hearts—the decision to silence the world's lies that our imperfect homes aren't enough and trust that God can use our table, in all its imperfection, to reveal more of who he is.

Preparing to Welcome Others

If you are not born with expertise in something, it takes effort to develop your skills and become proficient. You must commit to practicing that discipline daily. Committing to daily preparation to open your heart and show love through hospitality shouldn't be overlooked.

Let's think about it this way.

A new family has moved in on your street, and you

The Preparation

decide to invite them over for dinner. You spend hours ironing your linens for the table, hand-kneading a sourdough pie crust and braiding the edges, dusting every baseboard, and even going so far as to plant fresh perennials in the front yard. Your home is inviting and welcoming. It looks immaculate and straight from a magazine and smells heavenly as you open the door for your new neighbors.

What I have just described is not hospitality in the biblical sense. What I have just described is textbook for entertainment, worldly hospitality.

I'm not saying that cleaning your house or preparing exquisite food *can't* be part of biblical hospitality. If you desire to show love through a clean house or a freshly baked pie, then your heart is in the right place. However, if you are grumbling while on your knees cleaning the baseboards or thinking about how impressed someone will be with your baking skills while you artfully braid the crust, you might need to do a check and ensure your heart is prepared to welcome people in.

Preparing to welcome people doesn't require a formal invitation. It can happen spontaneously on a regular Tuesday. Our goal should be to live so closely aligned with God's will that our homes, our tables, our pantries, and our hearts are prepared to open the door any day of the week.

The invitation doesn't have to be polished or planned out. "I would love to invite you and your family over for dinner on Friday night." It can be as simple and warm as "Pop on over! My door is always open. In fact, why don't you stay for dinner?" That kind of everyday, come-as-you-are welcome reflects the heart of true hospitality.

Tim Chester described it like this: "Elaborate dinner parties can easily become hospitality as performance. They promise intimacy but can, in fact, maintain distance through formality. The focus of entertaining is impressing others; the focus of true hospitality is serving others."[3] This is the heart of it: Hospitality isn't about impressing people. It's about loving them.

The preparation of our heart requires us to throw off the comparison game with the world and lean into the beauty of imperfect, intentional connection. It calls us to say, "Yes, my home is messy, and I might not have enough food, but I know God will meet us here." The dishes don't need to match, the décor doesn't have to be Instagram-worthy, and the meal doesn't need to be gourmet. What truly matters is showing up with love and making space for people. If we want to follow Christ's example, we can start by simply being ready: Ready to open the door. Ready to serve. Ready to trust that God shows up in the ordinary, everyday moments when we choose to love like him.

How to Prepare Your Heart

Preparing our hearts before preparing our homes is vital, because true biblical hospitality flows from a genuine desire to serve others just like Jesus did. If our hearts are restless, anxious, or overly focused on appearances, we may inadvertently turn hospitality into a performance rather than an authentic invitation to experience Christ at the table. But when we invite the Holy Spirit to guide us, we start to

The Preparation

see others the way he does. This helps us embrace everyone with love and kindness, free from judgment or pride. It's a beautiful way to connect with people just as they are!

Consider this: How would our gatherings shift if, before setting the table, we asked God to remove distractions from our minds and help us see the people he has placed in our lives with his compassion and wisdom? When we approach hospitality with a prepared heart, our focus naturally shifts from impressing others to truly blessing them. It transforms our homes into a place where all are welcome and all can experience the true connection that comes only from God.

This heart preparation calls us to pray for a spirit of peace, to release any lingering anxieties, and to listen deeply to what the Holy Spirit may want to do through us. It's about surrendering our expectations and allowing God to move in our interactions. We may find that when we focus on heart preparation, even an early morning coffee or quick afternoon chat can turn into soul care that sparks a deeper intimacy with Jesus through genuine friendship.

Let's explore how to prepare our hearts and open our homes in ways that foster not only connection but also the spiritual encouragement that anchors our hospitality. With God at the center, hospitality becomes more than a performance; it becomes a gift that invites his presence into every moment.

1. Create a Habit of Prayer

To make prayer a part of our lifestyle, it needs to be a priority, which means being intentional about protecting time spent with God. As a new mom, I have shifted my

Preparing Your Heart

daily prayer rhythms to fit this season of life. Being deliberate about carving out time for prayer in the morning, before everyone else wakes up, helps safeguard that special moment with God so I don't let the day slip away from me. This means getting up early to give myself plenty of time to spend with the Lord. Maybe for you it looks like setting up consistent time on your calendar to stop and spend time with God. Or maybe it looks like keeping a small journal that has short prayers written in it that you repeat throughout the day.

We know that prioritizing prayer is important because it was one of the habits Jesus practiced during his ministry. Mark 1:35 says, "Very early in the morning, while it was still dark, Jesus got up, left the house and went off to a solitary place, where he prayed." His habit of prayer empowered him to connect with his Father and do what the Father called him to do. In the same way, prayer helps us center our hearts and our minds on displaying God's love to those around us through hospitality.

In its simplest form prayer is a conversation with God, which is cool because when we are trying to be more like him, we need to hear from him. And we cannot expect to hear from God without first starting the conversation.

What do you want me to do in this situation?
What are you trying to teach me?
How can I be more like you?
Who should I invite over?

When seeking God through prayer, we must also be open to changing ourselves based on how God responds and who he places on our heart. Incorporating prayer into our busy lives can sometimes feel a bit overwhelming, but it doesn't have to be! Remember, prayer isn't limited to formal settings or lengthy silences. Instead, we can easily weave prayer into our everyday routines in simple and meaningful ways.

Think about turning those mundane moments into special ones: Whisper a quick prayer while doing the dishes, take a moment to express gratitude while waiting in line, or breathe a prayer of comfort when you're feeling anxious.

Spontaneous prayers throughout the day can be a wonderful way to invite God into your daily activities and choices. These little conversations remind us that prayer isn't just another task on our to-do list; it's a beautiful dialogue with someone who loves us deeply. You might even find it helpful to set reminders on your phone or leave little sticky notes with prayer prompts around your space.

The goal is connection. When we embrace the opportunity to pray in those often-overlooked moments, we create a habit of inviting God into our lives. It transforms prayer from a chore into a lifeline, helping us stay present and in tune with God's voice even amid the chaos of daily life. So embrace the chance to chat with God in your own unique way and watch how this practice deepens your walk with him and draws you into the discipline of hospitality.

2. Small Moments Add Up; Use Them Wisely!

We would also be wise to put to good use the time we've been given to serve God. While we may not magically gain additional hours in the day, we can embrace the small moments that fill our weeks. It's easy to feel overwhelmed by the thought of being hospitable, especially if it seems like a big, daunting task. But remember, even the smallest acts can be profound!

Consider how little moments can compound into something beautiful. Maybe you have a spare five minutes before dinner; use that time to set your table, whether it's with your finest china or simple paper plates. Just having that space ready can transform your home into an inviting atmosphere, making it easier to say yes when someone drops by.

At the end of each day, take a few moments to tidy up your living space. You don't have to do a deep clean every night, but if everyone pitches in to pick up their things, wipe down the counters, and put away the dishes, you'll wake up to a welcoming environment. This simple routine sets the stage for spontaneous gatherings and makes it less stressful when the Lord nudges you to open your door and welcome others in.

By integrating these small practices into the spare moments throughout your week, you're not just preparing your home; you're preparing your heart to reflect God's love. Each little effort adds up, turning your space into a haven of connection and warmth where everyone feels valued and welcomed. Trust that God will honor your faithfulness in these little things, and soon you might find that opening your door to others feels not only natural but a joyous expression of his love.

3. Start a List of People to Invite Over

It's important to remember that it's God's job to place specific people in our lives for us to invite over, and he's

The Preparation

faithful to provide everything we need to love on those people. Just as he entrusts us with resources to steward, he also entrusts us with his people to show hospitality toward. And we are called to cultivate a welcoming heart and home that reflect his love. But it can feel a bit overwhelming to scan our Facebook friends or contacts list in our phones and consider who to invite.

It's easy to get caught up in our doubts and worries. *She has four kids. That friend is taking night classes. I couldn't possibly invite that new couple; they'd think I'm weird!* But what if we shifted our mindset? What if, instead of worrying about the what-ifs, we began to see invitations as opportunities? God places people in our lives for a reason, and sometimes all it takes is one simple invite to build a lasting connection. Saying yes to the nudge from God to reach out to someone new could just be the opportunity God has been waiting for to answer your prayers!

Here are some practical tips to help you prepare yourself for hospitality:

- **Keep a running list of names** in your planner or on your phone of people you'd like to invite over. Jot down names whenever someone comes to mind: friends, acquaintances, or even new neighbors.
- **Set reminders** in your phone's Calendar or Reminders apps to prompt you every week or month to reach out to someone on your list. A gentle nudge can help turn your thoughts into action.
- **Match interests** by thinking about potential connections. If someone loves gardening, invite them over for

Preparing Your Heart

tea and to chat about plants. This not only gives the invitation a personal touch but gives you something to talk about if conversation gets awkward.
- **Ask for recommendations** from your close friends and family on how to pursue this desire to be more hospitable. They might suggest people you haven't considered, broadening your circle of potential guests. Maybe you and your girlfriends could cohost a themed dinner party and invite the couple who is new to your church.
- **Pray for guidance** about who God wants you to invite. You might be surprised at who he brings to your mind! This also prepares your heart to be open and receptive when opportunities arise.

I've started using the Reminders app to remind me to text someone who has been on my mind that day. Does this ever happen to you? You'll be driving from one place to the other or walking down the cereal aisle at the grocery store, and someone random pops into your mind. There isn't a bone in my body that believes this is random. I truly believe that is the Holy Spirit nudging you to reach out to that person. Oftentimes I don't reach out, because I'm in the middle of something or in transition from point A to point B. A simple reminder every day at 2:30 p.m. prompts me to text someone I thought of earlier. After having this reminder in my phone for well over two years, I don't really need it anymore. At 2:30 I will send a simple text to someone almost without thinking. It's wild how our minds create new pathways to form habits!

The Preparation

4. Look for Ways to Be Obedient

You can read a hundred books about preparing your heart and being obedient to Christ, but unless you put them into action, you won't get to experience more of him in a new and intimate way.

So what does obedience look like in the context of preparing our hearts for a life devoted to extending hospitality? It's a daily journey of realigning our lives with truth, and it begins with small, consistent steps that refocus us and remove the distractions and excuses in our lives. I love the three steps John Piper preached on obedience; they are like a road map that encourages us to invite the Spirit into our daily lives.[4]

1. **Don't ignore Scripture.** The Bible is God-breathed and should be respected as the final and decisive authority to our lives, including in the formation of our habits. We should be seeking truth in Scripture daily. This doesn't have to be a long and drawn-out task—maybe just a few minutes in the morning reading a devotional or listening to an audiobook on your way to or from work. The key here is consistency. When we saturate ourselves in truth from God's Word, we lay the foundation for everything else we do.
2. **Rely on truth.** As we soak in the Scriptures, we find that our habits begin to reflect divine truths. I know you have heard the saying "What goes in, comes out." Or the proverb "For as he thinketh in his heart, so is he" (Prov. 23:7 KJV). When we focus on truth, we

can avoid getting caught up in the distractions and excuses of this world.

Imagine the shift in perspective you will have when you begin to let God's Word influence your approach to hospitality. John Piper puts it like this: "Think with the mind of Christ and assess things the way Christ would assess them so that the decisions that are made really are flowing from the revealed will of God in the Bible as it transforms your mind."[5] Rather than seeing hospitality as a chore and a stressor, choose to see it as a joyful expression of your obedience to Christ.

3. **Embrace spontaneity.** When our lives start to reflect these truths, hospitality becomes more spontaneous. It's the unexpected Tuesday night invite that makes people feel valued, seen, and loved. Think about it. How special does it feel when someone reaches out without an agenda, just to share time together?

That kind of spontaneous invitation is only possible when we slow down enough to cultivate a habit of inviting others in. When this becomes second nature, we start to notice the divine placements of people in our lives and recognize those moments when we can serve and love others intentionally.

As you reflect on what obedience means in your life, keep in mind that it's not about being perfect; rather, it's about making steady progress toward God's intentions. When we prepare our hearts to align with him, we foster a spirit of hospitality that can transform not only our own

The Preparation

lives but also the lives of those we encounter. Let's remain open and attentive, ready to embrace the beautiful and chaotic moments God has in store for us!

● ● ● ● ● ●

In a world that's all about instant results, praying and asking the Lord for guidance doesn't always get you an instant answer. Friend, don't be discouraged. Use these seasons of waiting as a time to actively prepare for hospitality. You might not sense God's nudge to invite someone over or even know who to invite, but that doesn't mean you order takeout, ignore the invite, and sit back and wait.

Allow God to use quiet seasons to develop your hospitality muscles. From cooking to keeping your home tidy to creating conversations around faith, these are muscles you can always be developing. When we wait patiently for God to use us, he will strengthen us and be faithful to develop us.

Preparing the heart can be challenging because it takes our sinful inclinations and rewires our habits to reflect Christ. This type of living is completely countercultural. Once we prepare our hearts, then everything else flows from it.

Part 2
The Invitation

Chapter 5

• • • • • •

The Excuse You're Making

After I finished speaking at a church in Paragould, Arkansas, an older woman approached and told me she loved that I'd written a cookbook, but she wouldn't be taking one because hospitality wasn't her spiritual gift. It wasn't until I was reflecting on that moment later that the light bulb went off for me. Building your community isn't about having the spiritual gift of hospitality. It's about loving and serving others. Regardless of the season we're in, the most meaningful thing we can do is be ourselves and show love to others, whether through grand gestures or small acts of kindness that can make a big difference.

I don't know about you, but I crave deep connection. Unfortunately, it can be extremely difficult to cultivate.

The Invitation

Finding friends is almost as hard as navigating without Google Maps in a foreign country; you are just living on hope and prayer. Where do we turn when we're unsure how to create community? Where do we start?

Let me tell you where not to turn: anywhere that pressures you to be perfect. Remember that spiritual gifts are traits you're born with, so they come naturally. Spiritual disciplines require time and practice to develop. I discovered that the key to discipline lies in unwavering focus and persistent effort, even in the face of setbacks. Think about it: When someone prepares for a race, they don't just go to the track, flippantly run a couple laps, and then wing the race. They have an intense and focused training schedule. They're disciplined not only in their mindset to run a long distance but also in the preparation it will take for them to complete their goal.

Just as when training for a race, we need to be focused with the spiritual disciplines. First Timothy 4:7 says you should "discipline yourself for the purpose of godliness" (NASB). That is the race we're running, the goal we're chasing—godliness. And practicing hospitality can help us.

Have you found yourself alone and needing community? Maybe that is why you picked up this book. If you don't feel super connected to people or you're just unsure about inviting people into your space, you are not alone. The United Kingdom created a position called the minister of loneliness in 2018 because an overwhelming percentage of the British population had identified as lonely.[1] They wanted to fix this problem. This was before the pandemic, when the required isolation really made people lonely. Then in 2021, the UK

The Excuse You're Making

started a campaign called Better Health—Every Mind Matters. It targeted millennials and Gen Z, encouraging them to fight loneliness by having intentional conversations with someone or inviting people out for tea or coffee.[2]

Sounds familiar, right? Our world is craving connection, and how is it prescribing to fix the problem? Hospitality. One small step at a time.

We must build a deep, God-centered community with those who will hold us accountable, pray for us, check in on us, show up for us, and, most importantly, encourage us.

Building this type of community can be extremely intimidating and overwhelming, especially for the introverts in the room. And when we think about not just asking someone to grab coffee but instead inviting them into our home where we might be providing the coffee, it can get even more intimidating.

Imagine hospitality as a practice rather than a performance, as something that grows easier with gentle repetition. Instead of a big event or perfect meal, think of hospitality as simply making space for others. Starting small allows you to focus less on impressing and more on connecting, shifting the pressure from perfection to presence. And like any habit, the more you practice, the more natural it becomes. With time, you'll see that you don't need expertise to foster connection—just a bit of consistency and a welcoming heart. If we can identify what is holding us back from opening that door, I guarantee God will show up and help us remove that barrier. Then you'll see how rewarding genuine intimacy with him and others can be.

If you had to put pen to paper, what would you say

The Invitation

is keeping you from creating a habit of hospitality? What intimidates you about inviting people in? Is it your home? Your cooking abilities? Maybe you've seen a friend or even your family do it well, and the pressure to measure up is overwhelming. Or maybe your life is chaotic, running from soccer practice to the gym to school pickup, and adding one more thing to your busy plate seems impossible.

I feel all of these for you, and I've experienced most of them too. I've even added a few of my own excuses to the list from time to time.

What's Your Excuse?

Why do you think we make excuses for something that will have so many benefits? They often hold us back from experiencing all that life has to offer. Many of us can relate to the excuses that keep us from pursuing a rhythm of hospitality, and we should consider how our pride may be at the root of all of them. Instead of focusing inward on what our excuses are—"I'm too busy," "I'm not a good host," "I haven't had time to clean the house"—we should look outward and have a heart for the people around us, as God intended.

The world loves to place unattainable standards on us, to pressure us into fitting into a box we weren't created to fit into. And do you know what happens when we try? We become defeated, because we're trying to live up to a standard we can't ever meet, a game we won't ever win—on purpose. We weren't created in God's image to fit into the world's boxes. The world's standards are designed to keep us striving without ever allowing us to truly rest, leaving us perpetually feeling like we're falling short and never enough. But because we are made in the image of God, his plan for us is bigger than the world's expectations. He created us with purpose, not to conform to fleeting standards but to reflect his love and grace in everything we do. Bottom line: That hamster wheel we're on, chasing the world's standards, makes us aimless, lacking true direction and losing sight of God's purpose for our lives.

Excuses become an easy fallback, a way to protect ourselves from the failure we fear will come if we try something and then fall short. But all that does is trap us in inaction, keeping us from stepping out in faith and experiencing the blessings that come when we trust God over the world. The truth is, God is bigger than the unattainable standards the world tries to set for us, and when we focus on him instead, we'll discover the true purpose and freedom we've been searching for.

Jesus was our example of how to build our community on earth. While he was God, he was also fully man, and we can learn how we should build our community through his social interactions with his disciples, his family, and strangers he met while passing through towns on his travels. Jesus provides an example of this bring-your-whole-self-to-the-table mentality that we are yearning for.

So how—amid the chaos, the unattainable standards, and the overwhelming pressures of our culture—do we put in the practice and discipline of cultivating a spirit of hospitality?

The Invitation

We need to face the facts: The hesitation we feel around hospitality often comes down to making excuses. Most of us have been there, justifying why now isn't the right time to open our homes or connect with others more deeply. We convince ourselves it's our messy house, lack of cooking skills, or simply our overwhelming schedule. But when we strip these excuses away, we're often just holding back from the blessings God has for us through meaningful relationships. Hospitality is about showing up authentically and making room for others, just as Jesus did. The truth is, our excuses keep us from experiencing the richness of life that God wants to give. Let's identify the barriers that hold us back, address them head-on, and start reaping the blessings that a spirit of welcome brings. It's time to stop holding back and start opening up.

"But I have no clue where to start."

Don't be too hard on yourself if you don't get it right the first time. Instead, embrace the learning process and keep going. Start by inviting one or two people over for coffee or a casual lunch, rather than planning a full meal or party. Choose a day and a time that feel easy for you, and set a relaxed tone by letting guests know it's informal—no need for elaborate prep work.

As someone who has written a cookbook and loves being in the kitchen, my instinct is to encourage you to prepare a favorite snack or simple treat—something you're comfortable with, maybe even a charcuterie board. But let's be honest: Cooking is not everyone's thing, and charcuterie can be even more intimidating than inviting someone

The Excuse You're Making

over! So here is my encouragement and my permission to do something simple:

- Purchase a box of cookies, a loaf of dessert bread (lemon or chocolate are always crowd-pleasers), or just pop a bag of popcorn and put it in a fun bowl with some candy on top.
- Invite people over for dinner but tell them to bring their dinner. I'll let you in on a little secret: This is my go-to hospitality hack. I am the poster child for inviting people over and telling them to BYOF (Bring Your Own Food). And guess what? People will do it! They don't want to eat alone just as much as you don't.

The goal isn't to impress; it's to connect. Ask thoughtful questions, listen well, and keep the focus on enjoying each other's company. If starting a conversation seems like a tall order, pick up a pack of conversation starters and let everyone pick a card and read a question.

As you build confidence with these small steps, hospitality will start to feel more natural, and you'll see how impactful it can be to invite others in and how little prep work you actually need.

With dedication and consistency, you'll soon find yourself with a desire to create more moments of hospitality than there are days in the week. God designed us to do hard things, and he promises in Scripture not to give you more than you can handle (Ps. 55:22; Isa. 41:10; 1 Cor. 10:13; Phil. 4:13). You've got this!

The Invitation

"What do I even make? I don't know how to cook, and I've never been good at following recipes."

You are in great company! I may have written a cookbook and have a hospitality blog, but I didn't always know how to cook. In fact, I used to feel completely out of my element in the kitchen. I'd open a recipe and find myself overwhelmed by the terminology and list of endless ingredients. I worried that if I didn't get every step perfect, the dish would be a disaster. To be honest, I'm not good at following recipes, so using an involved twelve-step recipe was a hard pass for me—too overwhelming! But I learned that just like hospitality, cooking isn't about perfection; it's about showing up, trying new things, and doing it with love.

These are my tried-and-true reminders that cooking doesn't have to be intimidating.

- **Start small and simple.** Don't feel pressured to dive into complicated recipes. Begin with a few basic, foolproof dishes, like a comforting soup (broth, veggies, and a few herbs), a hearty pasta (a jar of sauce, your favorite pasta shape, and maybe a protein), or my favorite, turkey and cheese crescent roll-ups. If you know me, you know I couldn't suggest recipes without at least one involving crescent rolls. Do yourself a favor and always keep crescent rolls in your fridge. Recipes with fewer steps are harder to mess up and will build your confidence. Focus on flavors you enjoy and remember that every cook starts somewhere.
- **Practice with your go-to ingredients.** Choose a handful of versatile ingredients—like garlic, olive oil,

herbs, and a few favorite vegetables—and learn to use them well. Mastering a few ingredients gives you flexibility and makes cooking feel less overwhelming. You'll soon find that you can create variations with just a few adjustments, adding depth to your meals without feeling like you're starting from scratch each time.

One of my favorite ways to practice with herbs and discover which ones I enjoy is to make an olive oil dip. You know the kind served at fancy Italian restaurants? I like to serve it on a charming appetizer plate, alongside a fancy loaf of store-bought bread. It makes me feel sophisticated, even though all I'm really doing is tearing into some bread and sprinkling herbs into olive oil. In my opinion, the best herbs for olive oil dipping are garlic (of course!), thyme, tarragon, and basil. I recently found a delightful basil salt, and I highly recommend Trader Joe's 21 Seasoning Salute; it's a must-have seasoning that I keep on hand at all times. It's perfect for proteins, veggies, and olive oil dips, and it adds an elegant touch to the presentation of cheese on a charcuterie board.

- **Embrace mistakes as learning.** Mistakes are part of the journey in the kitchen, and even the most experienced chefs will tell you they've had their share of culinary mishaps. When you embrace mistakes as a chance to learn, you free yourself from the fear of failing. If you burn a dish or end up with mushy pasta, don't be discouraged. Instead, take a moment to reflect on what happened: Was the heat too high,

The Invitation

or did the food need more time? Use that experience as a guide for next time.

Remember, cooking doesn't need to be serious, and even mistakes can add joy to your meal. Burnt toast or overly salted soup can become part of a funny story that adds conversation and connection to the table. Even though my great-grandmother passed away when I was three, my family still talks about how she burned literally every roll she put in the oven. She was known for taking a serrated knife and scraping off the char from burnt biscuits before serving them. In fact, she did it so frequently, my grandfather thought that was just how biscuits were served for the better part of his childhood. Let yourself enjoy cooking, mistakes and all!

I know those mistakes can seem disheartening, especially if you're a perfectionist, but don't forget to give yourself the freedom to play around. Try adding a new spice or switching up cooking times to see what you like. Every time you try something new with a recipe, you learn a little bit more about the cooking process, and it becomes more fun.

Cooking is creative; it's not a strict science. Except for baking. Baking is a science, so don't be afraid to stick with store-bought mixes or slice-and-bake cookies. Each mistake made while cooking is a step closer to the confidence and joy you'll feel as you find your rhythm in the kitchen. Every imperfect meal still carries the warmth and intention of hospitality, and your willingness to learn is what makes each dish special.

The Excuse You're Making

By starting with simplicity and consistency, you'll build a rhythm that feels natural and you'll begin to feel more confident. Soon enough, cooking will become an extension of yourself and your hospitality. And remember, it's not about the skill but the heart behind the meal. You're welcoming others in and serving them with love, which matters far more than a perfectly executed recipe.

"I have kids, no time, and no energy to be hospitable."

In the middle of soccer practices, band concerts, and church events—and don't forget time to relax and recharge—it can be hard to spontaneously invite people in. It doesn't have to happen tomorrow or even next week, but it will never happen if you don't plan it.

So pick a date, invite a couple of people over, and make a plan. It will get easier the more times you do it. I promise. Just imagine the joy and laughter that will fill the room as you serve delicious food, share stories, and connect with your people.

Here are a few things that have helped me with planning:

1. **Always keep a journal or make notes.** To make your hospitality experience a success, keep track of recipes that work well for a crowd. This can make inviting a group of people over more attainable and boost your culinary confidence—even if your note says: "Pick up a party platter from Walmart!"
2. **Keep it simple.** Having a list of quick meal ideas and pantry staples to keep on hand makes last-minute meals with friends simple. This will take the stress

The Invitation

out of spontaneity and give you the opportunity to focus on the people.
3. **Create checklists of tasks that need to be done every time you host.** This can help you stay organized and reduce stress. That way, you can focus on enjoying the company of your guests and creating memorable experiences.

MY MENTAL CHECKLIST

Some things on here won't apply to your space or every invitation you extend, but hopefully this will be a great starting point for you to create your own checklist.

1. **Tidy up.** Do a quick tidy of the main living area, kitchen, and bathroom. I like to make sure the sink is clean and the countertops have been wiped off.
2. **Get a drink ready.** Put out glassware and pour a pitcher of water or brew fresh coffee, depending on time of day and weather, so it's ready for guests. This is also a great reminder for me to offer my guests a drink after welcoming them inside. For some reason, I always forget to offer a drink to people, so having it out on the counter reminds me to ask if they'd like something.
3. **Light the candles.** Try to light a candle in the bathroom, kitchen, and entryway. I'm a big candle girly; they just make everything feel a bit more homey.

4. **Prepare snacks.** I don't always have snacks out; it depends on the time of day and what I've invited people over for. I do have an epic snack drawer, though—we love snacks at my house—so if I haven't prepared something and guests request a snack, I can pull out chips, granola, crackers, whatever. We also keep a massive two-gallon glass jar full of trail mix next to some cute decorative bowls, and this is always a fan favorite for snacking.
5. **Clean the bathroom.** Ensure the bathroom is clean and stocked with toilet paper, soap, and a hand towel.
6. **Set the table.** Set the table with everything ahead of time. If we are eating a meal, I prefer to serve from the table instead of the kitchen. If you are waiting for food to come out of the oven at the last minute, hold a place on the table with a potholder or trivet so you know exactly where to place it when it comes out of the oven. And don't forget about serving utensils. You can lay those on the table next to where the food will go when you set the table ahead of time.
7. **Turn on some music.** Play soft background music to create a relaxed atmosphere.
8. **Open the curtains.** Allow natural light to enter and brighten the space. Natural light is known to have a calming effect on our nervous system. A well-lit room filled with sunlight can create a serene and inviting atmosphere, fostering relaxation and open communication. It can also make a home feel more authentic and personal, enhancing the sense of belonging and comfort.

9. **Check the temperature.** Don't forget to periodically ask how your guests feel temperature-wise in your home. This is the last thing I do, because I am a hot box. I love my 65-to-68-degree home, but historically, my guests prefer my home around 72 degrees. About twenty minutes before people arrive, I turn the thermostat up. However, I always have blankets available for those who are still chilly.
10. **Read up on hosting tips and tricks in the back of the book.** I've included countless resources to help you become a better host and create unforgettable experiences for your guests.

◇◇◇◇◇◇◇◇◇◇◇◇◇◇◇◇◇◇◇◇◇◇◇◇◇◇◇◇◇◇◇◇◇◇◇◇

"My house is so small, I can't bring anyone into it. I don't even have a table!"

Thinking that your home is too small to invite people in is a common concern, but it doesn't have to be a barrier to hospitality. Remember, this isn't about the size of your space; it's about the warmth and connection you create with others. A cozy environment can actually foster deeper conversations and meaningful connections. When Kyle and I got married, we didn't have a table for the first ten months, and we used different-sized TV trays and sofa tables for our guests. Get creative when you are inviting people over!

Here are a few practical ways to think outside the box and host gatherings in smaller spaces:

The Excuse You're Making

1. Consider the idea of a **casual, stand-up gathering** instead of a sit-down dinner. You don't need a formal dining table to entertain. Instead, arrange a few chairs or cushions around your living room or create a cozy corner. Encourage guests to mingle and chat, serving light snacks or finger foods that don't require cutlery or sitting down: platters of cheese, crackers, and fruits or a selection of appetizers that guests can easily grab while they chitchat with each other. This informal setup can lead to a relaxed atmosphere where people feel free to move and interact.

2. Another option is to host a **themed gathering** with a specific focus that requires minimal space. Consider a book club, movie night, or game night. Set up a small area with comfortable seating and gather around for a fun activity. Encourage everyone to bring their favorite snacks to share, which not only lightens your load but also makes everyone feel included. You can create a cozy, welcoming vibe by dimming the lights and using some soft pillows and blankets, transforming your small space into an inviting haven for connection.

3. Don't overlook the potential of **outdoor spaces** if you have access to a balcony, patio, or backyard. An outdoor setting can make any small gathering feel spacious and open. Set up a few chairs or a picnic blanket, hang some string lights, and enjoy the fresh air. If it's chilly, consider providing blankets and a small firepit for warmth. This change of scenery can

The Invitation

lift the spirit of your gathering, allowing everyone to relax and enjoy each other's company.

When you are creating a habit of hospitality, the key is to shift your mindset from seeing your space as a barrier to recognizing it as an opportunity to invite people in and show Christ's love to them. Embrace the coziness of your home, focus on the people you invite, and prioritize the experiences you create together. With a little creativity, your small space can become a place where people feel welcomed and the conversation goes deep. And in my opinion, that's when God does his best work.

"People will laugh at the way I plate things. I don't have special plates or cups, and my silverware is mismatched!"

If mismatched silverware and an eclectic mix of plates and glasses are holding you back from inviting others over, let's tackle that mindset together. Your guests are there to connect with you, not critique your dinnerware. A laid-back atmosphere can make people feel more at ease, knowing they're in a real home with real people. There's a certain charm in a mismatched table setup, and with a little creativity, you can make it feel intentional and cozy.

One of the easiest ways to simplify is to go with disposable dinnerware. I love how creative paper and disposable plate companies have become over the years, especially around holidays. A set of matching paper plates and cups can add a pop of personality to your table and save you from washing dishes. Look for styles that fit your personality or the theme of the evening—everything from florals to bold patterns or seasonal designs. You can even find fun plastic glassware with gold rims for an elegant touch without the cost of fine china. Sophistiplate, for example, offers a wide selection of beautiful disposable options, from plates and napkins to forks and spoons, making it easy to add flair to your table without any stress. You get the satisfaction of a put-together look while keeping things simple and budget friendly.

If you're feeling creative, why not set the table with a mix of what you already have? Embrace the beauty of different colors, shapes, and styles. If you own a variety of mugs, glasses, or small bowls, consider assigning each one to a different guest for a fun, personalized touch. And don't worry about achieving a formal place setting—a simple arrangement is just as charming. Just place a fork, knife, and napkin at each setting, allowing room for your own creative flair. Remember, the warmth of the meal and the joy of conversation will always matter more than what the table looks like.

The beauty of hospitality is in bringing people into your space, however it looks, and offering them connection and care. So pick up some disposable plates if that's easiest, or mix and match with what you have and enjoy the relaxed, personal touch it brings. Your guests will remember the experience of being together far more than they'll remember the plates or glasses on the table.

"Having people over is way too expensive; I can barely afford my own groceries."

I feel you. It can be intimidating to buy extra food, prepare a meal, and open your home. What if I told you that

The Invitation

those excuses are how Satan wants you to view hospitality: as a burden and an unattainable rhythm that is impossible for where you are in life.

It's easy to conclude that hospitality requires this big budget with elaborate food, but that mindset shifts our focus from biblical hospitality to entertainment. When we see hospitality as a costly obligation, we begin to worry about impressing our guests rather than connecting with them. Biblical hospitality is about opening our hearts and homes with whatever we have, refocusing to the needs of others rather than the perfect presentation. It's the kindness of sharing a meal together, the warmth of making someone feel welcome, and the willingness to connect regardless of what's on the menu.

The story of the widow in 1 Kings 17:10–16 is a beautiful example of this. When Elijah arrived in Zarephath, he found a widow gathering sticks to prepare a meal. She had a handful of flour and a little oil left, only enough to feed herself and her son. Yet, when Elijah asked for a piece of bread, she didn't hesitate. Her willingness to share what little she had showed the heart of biblical hospitality.

God honored her faith, and her flour and oil never ran out. This story reminds us that hospitality isn't necessarily about abundance; it's about being willing to share. When we open our hearts, we create space for God to show up, and that's where true hospitality happens. And when we shift our perspective from the need to impress to the joy of serving, we can practice true hospitality in any setting and on any budget.

But how do you actually do that?

The Excuse You're Making

- **Potluck instead of catering:** One way to invite others in without overspending is to host a potluck-style gathering. Invite friends to each bring a dish to share, and keep it casual by asking for simple, affordable recipes. This not only lightens the financial load but also creates a sense of community, as everyone contributes something unique to the meal. Consider making a comforting, inexpensive main dish like a pasta bake, soup, or hearty salad that goes a long way and is easy to prepare in bulk. When each person brings a small dish, the focus is less on extravagance and more on the joy of sharing.
- **Snacks instead of the big meal:** You can also create a budget-friendly gathering by focusing on simple snacks or drinks instead of a full meal. Consider hosting a dessert night or a coffee gathering where each guest brings their favorite treat or just enjoys a cup of coffee together. A cozy setup with tea, coffee, and a few affordable baked goods can be just as meaningful as an elaborate dinner. Soft lighting sets the mood, and it's your genuine conversation and warmth that ensure guests feel welcome—not a lavish spread. Personally, I love inviting friends over for coffee and preparing a basket of store-bought mini muffins. I find a variety pack of twenty-four muffins for around five dollars, making it easy and stress-free. This approach keeps the focus on the people rather than the preparation, allowing me to focus on serving others.
- **Picnic instead of buffet:** Inexpensive gatherings can also extend outdoors or to community spaces. Host

a picnic or an outdoor potluck at a local park or in your backyard where everyone can enjoy the fresh air. Bring along some blankets and let guests know that it's a simple gathering; everyone can bring their own Chick-fil-A or just their Swig Dirty Soda and cookies.

Maybe you don't relate to any of these excuses. Honestly, I could write an entire book on excuses we make to keep our doors shut. I've heard things like, "My kids are too wild" or "I can't pay for a babysitter." Others have mentioned that their husband doesn't want to have people over or that they worry about what guests might think of their space. Then there are those who feel overwhelmed with their schedules or just say, "I'm way too busy." It's pretty common during the holidays to hear, "My house isn't decorated." And many feel uneasy about inviting people they don't know well. The list of excuses can get pretty long.

These excuses reveal the hesitation we often feel around hospitality, especially when it doesn't look like what we see on social media or when it challenges our comfort zone. We worry that our space isn't adequate, our food won't impress, or our lifestyle is too busy to add another commitment. But here's the truth: When we shift our mindset from entertaining to serving, these excuses lose their power, and we start to see that our willingness matters more than our resources.

Consider how Jesus extended hospitality: He didn't wait for ideal conditions or prepare an extravagant setting. His hospitality was rooted in love, compassion, and connection. Whether he was sharing meals with friends, strangers, or even those who disagreed with him, he consistently modeled a heart that welcomed others. By using what he had, wherever he was, he demonstrated that the essence of hospitality is not about impressing but about blessing. When we let go of our insecurities and invite people into our lives, we embody that same heart of Christ.

So let's set aside the excuses and ask ourselves what really matters. Is it a spotless home or a well-prepared meal? Or is it the warmth of connection, the joy of shared experiences, and the opportunity to reflect God's love through acts of kindness? Biblical hospitality calls us to look past the limitations and embrace the command to serve and love others intentionally.

Don't miss out on the community and connections you crave just because you're allowing excuses to hold you back. Hospitality can truly be life-altering, as it draws people deeper into an experience of God's kindness and faithfulness, inviting them to find rest in his provision. Don't let the Enemy convince you that you have nothing to offer. Embracing hospitality is one of the most powerful ways to share God's love, and each gathering becomes a chance for others to experience his grace through you.

Chapter 6

• • • • •

Go Ahead and Let the Biscuits Burn

Would you have guessed that hospitality is not my so-called spiritual gift? God gave me the gift of teaching and the gift of administration. I love finding God's winks in Scripture, explaining them, and providing context about them and helping others apply God's truth to their lives. I also thrive on creating plans and processes to organize people, thoughts, and ideas. However, I've come to value the importance of hospitality, because I saw a need for it. Just as my spiritual gift isn't hospitality, neither is prayer. But prayer is an important habit for my life. Through developing a consistent posture of prayer, I've

The Invitation

connected with God more, which allows me to understand him on a deeper, more intimate level.

Realizing what my spiritual gifts were didn't happen overnight, and it wasn't something I actively pursued. I had been serving with the students in my church for a few years before I realized I needed a community of people my own age. When I sought out this group of other single thirty-somethings, the church said they didn't have the capacity to create a ministry or space for us. I took it upon myself to address this gap in the church, which led me to discover my gifts in administration, teaching, and leading.

I wondered, *What would bring singles in their thirties together faster than anything else?* Food. So I decided to invite people to join me for a church service and lunch at my apartment afterward. I hosted my first gathering on Easter Sunday.

My family takes decorating and preparing for holidays very seriously, so I've always been one to go all out when it comes to celebrations. That Easter I dedicated a whole week to making sure my apartment and my dining table, which expanded to accommodate six people, were perfectly adorned. I even procured a succulent rack of lamb from my local butcher for my potential guests.

I had casually mentioned my plans to a few friends, thinking I might have three or four guests that Sunday. Boy, was I wrong! God had other plans, because twelve people ended up committing to celebrate Easter in my very small apartment. When I realized how many people were coming, I grabbed two card tables and some chairs from the church and stopped by the grocery store on the way home to stock up on microwavable sides and rotisserie chicken. Despite my surprise and overwhelm by the unexpected number of guests, the celebration was a lively and joyous gathering filled with laughter and good conversations.

However, amid all the hustle and bustle of creating the perfect ambiance, I lost sight of the true purpose of the lunch: to share the message of Jesus and find community. I had become so fixated on creating the ideal setting that I had overlooked the significance of connecting with the hearts of those who would be joining me at the table. Getting distracted by the ancillary details ultimately kept me from experiencing the blessings God wanted to give me when I invited people in. I've found blessings often come in unexpected ways, if I'm willing to stay flexible and open to his leading. While I was upset the card tables weren't decorated and we ended up eating the sides and chicken straight out of the grocery store containers, it ended up not mattering.

Looking back, I realized this event was my Mary-and-Martha moment. I was so focused on my rack of lamb and roasted brussels sprouts that I overlooked the people and the reason for our celebration: the resurrection of Christ. I had become like Martha when I desired to be like Mary. My intentions were pure. My desire for community was biblical. But my heart was focused on the desire for approval and perfection. There it was, looking me dead in the face: my pride.

Why do we hide behind our pride? I think it's because being vulnerable and living authentically is just plain hard—at least it is for me. Sharing the raw, messy parts of

The Invitation

our lives doesn't always come naturally. Honestly, it's easier to stay on the surface and keep things light and avoid the risk of going deep. Sometimes it even feels more fun that way. The truth is, our culture often pushes the idea that what people think of us matters more than being true to who God created us to be. It tells us to curate perfection instead of inviting people into our imperfections. And that kind of vulnerability? It can leave us feeling judged, inadequate, and discouraged. But if we let that fear dictate our actions, we end up holding back, keeping people at arm's length rather than welcoming them into our lives and homes. When we do that, we miss the chance to extend the kind of selfless, welcoming love the gospel calls us to.

It's natural to shy away from showing hospitality when we feel inadequate. But if we dig a little deeper, we might find that this fear of not being good enough can actually reveal an area of pride in our hearts. It sounds counterintuitive, but think about it: When we fixate on whether our home is tidy enough, our meal impressive enough, or our conversation engaging enough, we unintentionally place ourselves at the center of the equation. This mindset can quietly breed a sense of superiority, as if hospitality hinges on our ability to perform or meet some imaginary standard.

I know this struggle personally. When I first started out as a hospitality blogger and was promoting my cookbook, I felt this intense pressure to host elaborate, over-the-top themed parties, like I needed to become the next Martha Stewart to prove I was good at hospitality. I thought that if I could create picture-perfect gatherings, people would see me as an expert. But the more I chased that ideal, the more exhausted and disconnected I felt. Because that wasn't the kind of hospitality God was calling me to. He wasn't asking for over-the-top; he was asking me to create a space where the pomp and circumstance didn't matter—where the only thing that truly mattered was the invitation to the table.

The hard truth is, when we're consumed with proving our worth, we lose sight of the people standing right in front of us who God wants us to invite in. Pride isn't always loud and boastful. Sometimes it shows up as the quiet belief that everything rests on our shoulders. But biblical hospitality calls us to lay that down. It invites us to shift our focus from ourselves to the needs of others, trusting that God can work through our imperfections. Forming a habit of Christ-centered hospitality isn't about achieving perfection; it's about showing up, opening the door, and allowing God to cultivate a connectedness among us.

When we practice biblical hospitality, we put others' needs before our own. This outward focus not only blesses those we extend love to but also has the potential to bless us in return. God gives us each this beautiful opportunity to break down the barriers created by pride and self-centeredness and extend his grace and love to others, and in doing so, we all experience him in a new way.

Remember, cultivating a hospitable heart is a journey, and it's okay to acknowledge the battle of pride within your heart. Through small, intentional steps, we can gradually overcome this and open our hearts to others.

Setting aside pride is countercultural. Vulnerability is

attractive because it reflects genuine authenticity and invites trust. In a world that promotes curated perfection, people are drawn to those who are real and relatable. Authentic living resonates with our desire for connection; we crave relationships where we can be ourselves, flaws and all, without being judged. When we share our struggles and triumphs, we invite others to do the same, creating an atmosphere of belonging where people feel seen and understood. Ultimately, this honest exchange enriches our relationships and fosters a community rooted in compassion and love, and this openness is what we are striving for around our table.

As we reflect on our journey from being a Martha to embracing the spirit of Mary, it becomes clear that overcoming pride and accepting our imperfections—despite how vulnerable this may feel—is essential for becoming the Lord's hands and feet. By shifting our focus from ourselves to those we serve, we nurture a welcoming environment that fosters love and connection. This transformation goes beyond opening our homes; it involves opening our hearts to others in a way that mirrors Christ's love.

Embracing vulnerability opens the door to a more fulfilling life but requires intentionality and a shift away from the pressure of perfection. By allowing ourselves to be imperfect, we create a culture that celebrates authenticity over appearance. Prioritizing real connections over curated images fosters relationships that thrive on honesty and support. So how can we promote a vulnerable life? Here are some practical ways to cultivate that environment in our daily lives and pursue a life of vulnerable hospitality.

Let the Main Thing Be the Main Thing

Don't get wrapped up in the meal, the décor, or the environment. These are great things, but they're not hospitality. Instead begin shifting your mindset to the people; let them be the main thing. And if people are your focus, conversation with them will automatically become a priority. Conversation is the heartbeat of connection—a real-time exchange of thoughts, vibes, and stories that bridges gaps and builds relationships. It's more than just talking. It's the art of showing up, being present, and creating space for honesty, laughter, and those "me too" moments that make us feel seen. In a world of DMs and double taps, true conversation is the connection of the soul in face-to-face rhythms that reminds us we're not meant to do life alone.

However, conversation, especially the vulnerable kind, can sometimes feel intimidating. Opening up and letting people into our lives takes courage, but when we take that step of vulnerable obedience in conversation, the most meaningful connections are built. The next time you find yourself focusing on the details of the environment or the food and not the conversation and connection with your people, remember these three things:

1. **Prioritize.** Prioritizing meaningful and vulnerable conversation is at the heart of biblical hospitality. It's not just about inviting people into your home. It's about inviting them into your life. True connection happens when we slow down and make room for real conversations. Instead of rushing to clear the table or

jumping to the next activity, linger a little longer. Let the dishes wait. Rest in those moments of connection, where laughter, tears, and honest words build bonds that only grow through shared experiences. It's in those unhurried chats, where stories are told and hearts are opened, that we truly reflect the love of Christ. Don't forget to silence phones, turn off the TV, and keep devices out of sight to set the tone of conversation over distractions. This small step shows your guests that their presence is what matters most. You can also prioritize your time together chatting by arranging seating so people can face each other and talk more easily. Remember, it's the time spent together that truly matters, creating memories that will be cherished long after the dishes are done.

2. **Prepare.** Fostering genuine, healthy conversations is far more valuable than perfecting an elaborate five-course meal. Invest your prep time not just in the food but in setting the table for connection. Think through conversation starters that resonate with the people who will be there to encourage everyone to share beyond surface-level chatter. Set the tone early by welcoming guests with a deeper welcome than just an open door, letting them know you're glad they're there. A simple "I've been looking forward to this all day" can immediately make people feel more valued than a "Hey! Glad you are here." And finally, starting with prayer is probably my favorite way to begin a gathering, because it immediately lets everyone know that we are inviting God into the

moment and signals that this is a safe, intimate place for vulnerability and connection. When you prepare not just your home but your heart for meaningful conversation, you create an environment where people feel safe to be themselves, and it's in those honest, unguarded moments where true community is built, reflecting the heart of biblical hospitality.

3. **Practice.** Practicing good listening skills doesn't have to wait until you have guests over for dinner; it can start anywhere, at any time. Whether you're chatting with the barista at the coffee shop or the cashier at Target, take the opportunity to ask deeper questions and truly listen to their responses. It's about creating the habit of engaging with others in a way that shows you value what they have to say. Instead of sticking to surface-level small talk, ask about their day, their interests, or their thoughts on a topic, and really pay attention to their answers. The more you practice this kind of listening, the easier it becomes to carry this skill into your home and around your table. Soon you'll find that deep, meaningful conversation flows naturally, and it's not just something you try to do when hosting but becomes part of who you are in every interaction.

I want to be the kind of person who creates a safe space for others to open up and listens with empathy and understanding. Sharing our experiences and being vulnerable about what we've been through allows us to connect with others and share the provision and goodness of God with

The Invitation

those who may have never experienced him. God comforts us in our experiences so that we can, in turn, comfort others with the same love he has shown us (2 Cor. 1:3–4). Oswald Chambers once said, "If you are going to be used by God, he will take you through a multitude of experiences that are not meant for you at all. They are meant to make you useful in his hands."[1] He doesn't make us comfortable in our experiences; he makes us comfort-able—able to comfort others through our shared experiences.

It's the shared experience of divorce that can provide solace to a grieving wife. It's the support and encouragement shown from one mother—who has seen her wayward child come home—to another mother who is praying for her own child's return. It's the woman who is battling cancer with hope and peace that gives her the strength to walk through a diagnosis with someone else.

When you are vulnerable and welcome people to your table with shared experiences, you allow others to see the hope, grace, encouragement, and love they can find when we all come and sit at the table with Jesus. We are useful in his hands when we share who we are with one another. Try these things the next time you are connecting with someone:

1. **Practice reflective listening.** When someone opens up about their experiences or feelings, take a moment to reflect back what you've heard. For example, if a friend is talking about a tough situation at work, you might say, "It sounds like you're feeling really overwhelmed with all that pressure from your boss. That must be really tough." This shows that you're actively

listening and helps them feel validated in their emotions. Don't worry if your response isn't perfect or this feels awkward at first. What really matters is that you are interested in trying to understand what others are going through. Reflective listening helps build a stronger connection and encourages them to share even more, creating a safe space where being imperfect is okay.

2. **Ask open-ended questions.** Instead of sticking to yes-or-no questions, try asking open-ended ones to spark deeper conversations. If someone mentions they're dealing with a personal issue, you might say, "Can you share more about what that's been like for you?" This encourages them to share their story, giving you a better glimpse into their perspective. Open-ended questions create a safe space for vulnerability, which both makes it easier for others to share their experiences and shows that you genuinely care.

3. **Eliminate distractions.** To listen actively we need to carve out a distraction-free space. When you're in a conversation, try to put away your phone, turn off the TV, and really focus on the person in front of you. Show them they have your complete attention. If a friend starts sharing something personal, make sure to turn your body toward them, lean in a bit, and nod as they speak. This kind of body language demonstrates that you're present and interested in what they're saying. The goal is for you to be there for them and foster a safe, welcoming atmosphere where your friend feels comfortable opening up.

The Invitation

Wabi-Sabi

There is a Japanese philosophy that I find encouraging in creating a mindset that is focused on vulnerability. It's called wabi-sabi, and it "encourages us to appreciate that nothing is truly perfect or permanent."[2] Wabi-sabi is about appreciating the challenges and imperfections in life: the burned biscuits; the antarctic-like temperature of your home; the teeny, tiny table; or the lack of conversation skills you might have. In a world obsessed with curated perfection, we've become masters of illusion. We have become experts on how to present our lives with this glossy veneer that keeps every ounce of authentic living hidden. For so many of us, there is often a different story beneath the hard and, might I add, fake exterior we present. A story that is exhausted and depleted, longing for authentic connection with other believers that is built around communion with Jesus.

Instead of living trapped by the relentless pursuit of perfection, wabi-sabi teaches that we should accept ourselves and others and see things for how they truly are. And honestly, that mirrors what Scripture teaches. Now, I'm not saying Scripture is teaching that it makes no difference how you live as long you believe in Jesus. First Peter 4:3 clearly states that we need to flee the evil things that godless people enjoy, and Romans 13:13 commands us to live above reproach. But here is what is unique and beautiful about a relationship with Jesus: He doesn't demand perfection or even require it in order for us to be welcomed into his presence. He calls us to come just as we are, with all our imperfections, and promises to make our

Go Ahead and Let the Biscuits Burn

sins as white as snow. His invitation is open to everyone to come, sit at his feet, and drink deeply from the water of life. God isn't after our flawless performance; he's after hearts willing to walk in obedience, trusting that his grace is sufficient.

I remember hosting a dinner once where everything seemed to go wrong: The bread burned. I watered the centerpiece right before people came over, and the water leaked everywhere. And I dropped the unbaked pie and shattered the ceramic dish it was in moments before my friends were supposed to arrive. I wanted to cry, convinced the night was ruined. But as we gathered around the table, something beautiful happened during that imperfect evening. We laughed over the blackened bread, lingered longer in conversation, and shared stories of our own messiness. That evening I saw a glimpse of wabi-sabi hospitality—the beauty of connection thriving not despite the imperfections but because of them. It reminded me of how God welcomes us with open arms, ready to turn our broken moments into something divine.

I believe this is the intersection where wabi-sabi meets Christianity. Just as wabi-sabi recognizes the beauty of broken things, God acknowledges our brokenness and loves us through it. He doesn't discard us because of our failures. Instead, he redeems our mess and uses it for his glory. Our imperfections become testimonies of his grace and reminders that his strength is made perfect in our weakness.

It's not about our portrayed perfection; it's about saying yes to Christ no matter the chaos we find ourselves in

The Invitation

and extending grace-filled hospitality to those we encounter. When we do, we are putting God's glory on display by showcasing his love in the midst of our failures. We are taking the chaos, putting it to the side, and telling others that they are more important than the biscuits in the oven. You want to sit here with them. That, my friend, is where Jesus found Mary—on the floor with her guests. Even when there was stuff to do in the kitchen and around the house, she found the one important thing. Luke 10:42 says, "Mary has chosen the good portion, which will not be taken away from her" (ESV).

By acknowledging our imperfections and accepting our vulnerability, we can break down barriers keeping people we might not know from really opening up. This approach not only reflects our obedience to Christ but also creates a space where genuine relationships can be formed. Here are a few tips on how you can take these principles of wabi-sabi and foster genuine, Christ-centered connection.

1. **Embrace your imperfections.** Creating a welcoming home environment thrives in authenticity. Embrace the idea that minor messes, like scattered toys or unfolded laundry, are a natural part of everyday life. These little imperfections can actually make a space feel more lived in and relatable.
2. **Invite people in.** Opening your door more often, even when your space isn't tidy or fully ready, is a powerful way to cultivate connection. Be the home that has a revolving front door, where all are welcome no matter the state they are in or the state your home is

in. When we make this mindset shift, we welcome vulnerability and authenticity.
3. **Share your story.** Letting go of your picture-perfect image is a vital step toward becoming a true image-bearer of God. It can be easy to fall into the trap of projecting idealized versions of ourselves, but as followers of Christ, we are called to reflect his love and grace.

Being honest about our challenges can be incredibly liberating. For instance, you might share how you felt overwhelmed during a particularly tough week or how you've struggled with self-doubt in your role as a parent, a friend, or even a follower of Christ. These admissions resonate with others and signal that it's okay to be human. When we embrace our imperfections, we not only free ourselves from the burden of maintaining a false facade but we also reflect God's grace more clearly. God loves us in our messy, unrefined states, and he invites us to extend that same love to others.

Create Inviting Spaces

Kyle and I attended a premarital class at our church that was led by an amazing couple who epitomized humble hospitality. They really knew how to make everyone feel at home. They opened their doors to four couples every week, all while taking care of their six kids under age ten. And get this: Their house was just like any typical home with

The Invitation

kids running around and chores piling up. It was clean, but it wasn't sterile. It was welcoming and cozy, and when we walked in, we felt like family.

Kathryn and Josh could have easily shrugged off the prompting of the Holy Spirit to welcome four engaged couples into their home, because they felt their home wasn't perfect. Their kids weren't always quiet, and sometimes they were still eating dinner when we arrived. But they didn't let pride overcome the Holy Spirit's nudge. They understood that hospitality opens the door to vulnerability, and loving with the heart of Christ requires us to embrace that. Their openness and authenticity sparked some of the most meaningful and life-giving conversations as they helped prepare us for marriage.

Opening our spaces to people we don't know well can be intimidating, but when we find the courage to welcome people in, our vulnerability connects and binds us together. God created us to be people who crave community. Dr. Curt Thompson says it like this: "Yet it is only when we are known that we are positioned to become conduits of love. And it is love that transforms our minds, makes forgiveness possible, and weaves a community of disparate people into the tapestry of God's family."[3] When we gather around the table, willing to share not just our strengths but also our struggles, God uses that honesty to draw us closer to him and to one another.

But let's be real, vulnerability isn't always easy. When my house is messy or things feel out of order, I get uncomfortable, almost like my flaws are on display. It can make me question whether opening up is even worth it. As you prepare to welcome others, try not to overthink every detail, and don't be discouraged if they decline your invitation at first. Keep showing up, keep inviting, and trust that God is working through your willingness to open the door. If you do get discouraged, try these two things to make your invitation feel more natural:

1. **Host a cozy night.** Our culture has put pressure on not only the host but on the guests. When I am invited to someone's house, I wonder, *Do I need to take a hostess gift? Should I dress a certain way? Do I have to have it all together?* By hosting a cozy night you are encouraging everyone to be comfortable. You are allowing people the freedom to come as they are. What a relief! This is a great way to invite those who might feel overwhelmed by coming to your home or those you might not know well.

2. **Decorate with intent.** Decorating with throw pillows and stylish blankets may look great in a curated magazine spread, but that's not always reflective of real life. To create a functional and inviting space, consider personalizing your home with T-shirt blankets tossed in a large basket, photos of friends and family on display, or sentimental keepsakes that spark conversation. These touches not only make your home feel warm and welcoming but also showcase your unique story and encourage others to connect in personal ways.

The Invitation

Connection, Not Perfection

We've all scrolled through Instagram marveling at picture-perfect homes and gourmet meals. It's easy to think that our own lives don't measure up. But let's ditch the comparison game. Your home, with all its quirks and imperfections, is a unique and welcoming space.

I don't really struggle with my wardrobe on my own. That is until Instagram starts showing me endless posts of trendy women in stylish outfits, all telling me where to buy their clothes. Suddenly my closet feels inadequate. The thing is, if I didn't follow certain accounts, Instagram wouldn't have the power to make me feel this way. So I've had to mute or unfollow a few accounts and try to shift my algorithm, hoping to stop the constant reminders of clothes I don't actually need.

What do you see on Instagram? If you are inundated with accounts that show you what food to make, how to dress your table, or how to decorate your home so that you feel inadequate to invite people in, maybe it's time to take a look at what you are served or what you follow and how you can change that.

Remember, hospitality isn't about impressing others; it's about encouraging and edifying each other in truth and love. It's about creating a space where people feel safe to be themselves, where laughter and tears are shared, where lasting memories are made, and where Jesus wants to show up and love his people. By inviting people into your home to sit around your table, you are inviting them to experience Jesus in a deeper and more intimate way.

Here are a few things you can try as you begin to consider ways to focus on connection instead of perfection.

1. **Curate your feed.** Take time to review the accounts you follow on social media. Unfollow or mute those that contribute to feelings of inadequacy or comparison. Instead seek out accounts that inspire you, promote authenticity, encourage you to open your home just as it is, and point you back toward Jesus.
2. **Practice open-hearted invitations.** Make it a point to invite different people into your home regularly, whether they're neighbors, coworkers, or members of your church. By reaching out and getting to know people outside your inner circle, you increase the number of people you impact and begin to expand the ways in which you relate and share experiences with them.
3. **Storytelling sessions.** Host a storytelling night with friends where everyone can share personal stories. You might choose a theme—like travel adventures, childhood anecdotes, or the sketchiest restaurant that you'd visit again—or keep it open-ended. Be flexible with where the stories take you. Fostering conversation this way creates an intimate atmosphere that honors vulnerability and authenticity over aesthetics. This type of gathering not only deepens your relationship with others but also creates a memorable evening filled with laughter. Not to mention this is a great way to connect with people.

The Invitation

Hospitality isn't about putting on a show for others; it's about uplifting and supporting each other with your whole authentic self. I find this a bit freeing. I don't have it all together, and that's okay! God isn't asking me to; he's asking that my door stay open. Because when I invite people into my home to gather around my table, I'm giving them the chance to connect with Jesus in a more personal way.

So are you ready to drop the perfectionism and swing open your door? Let's celebrate the beauty of imperfect hospitality.

Chapter 7

• • • • • •

The Intentional Invitation

One of my dreams when I was growing up was to be athletic. I wasn't born with the height for basketball, the speed for track, or the coordination for tennis, but I carried a deep-seated desire to be part of a team. When it came time to pick teams in PE, I always hoped—sometimes prayed—to be chosen early. More often than not I stood there until the end, trying to look unbothered while my heart sank. It wasn't just about playing the game. It was about feeling seen and wanted. Isn't that what we all crave—to be chosen, to know we belong?

Invitations, whether to join a team or to sit around a table, shape our sense of belonging. They can create bridges of connection or reinforce invisible walls. Culturally, invitations are sometimes selective, extended based on social

The Invitation

status, convenience, or personal gain. They might come with subtle expectations or be used selfishly to boost one's social status or create personal opportunities rather than cultivate relationships. This kind of exclusivity can leave people feeling like they have to earn a place at the table. But true, intentional invitations break that cycle. They reflect the heart of biblical hospitality: an open-handed welcome that says, "You belong here just as you are." So who in your life is standing on the sidelines waiting for an invitation to belong?

Jesus exemplified this radical inclusivity—rooted in love—by inviting everyone to his table, whether they were wealthy or poor, respected or rejected, insider or outsider. The heart of biblical hospitality is to welcome others not for what they bring but because of who they are as loved and valued creations of God. This invitation extends beyond familiar social circles, reaching those who might otherwise be overlooked or marginalized. When Christians open their doors, the goal is to share life, hope, and the gospel, inviting all to belong to something greater than themselves. Unlike the invitations from the world, biblical hospitality is about meeting people where they are and offering them unconditional acceptance and love, mirroring the open arms of Christ.

I find it fascinating that from an early age, invitations are so important to us. I still remember the thrill of getting my first invitation to a birthday party in first grade. It was a brightly colored card with a picture of Simba and Nala on it, slipped into my cubby with my name carefully written on the front. I clutched that *Lion King*–themed card and read every detail over and over. Being invited meant I wasn't overlooked or forgotten; someone wanted me there. Isn't it funny how something as small as an invitation can make such a big impact? Can you think of a time when an invitation you received made you feel like you truly belonged?

Invitations are important because they satisfy our deep-rooted desire for connection, belonging, and purpose. At a fundamental level, an invitation is a gesture that says, "You are seen, wanted, and valued." Whether it's a simple invitation to coffee, a heartfelt invitation to dinner, or a formal invitation to a larger party, being invited reassures us that we are part of something beyond ourselves. Invitations hold the power to include us in moments, relationships, and experiences that enrich our lives and strengthen our sense of identity within a community or group of people. They are a bridge that helps us connect to others and find value and meaning in the things we associate with.

Invitations are meaningful because they create opportunities for growth and transformation. They allow us to step into new spaces, meet new people, and hear different perspectives. They also carry a deep significance, as they are a way to reflect God's open invitation to relationship. Every invitation we extend has the potential to cultivate a space for hope, healing, and unity, reminding us that we aren't meant to journey through life alone.

I have led several discipleship groups in women's ministries over the years. Different churches might call them different things—life groups, small groups, or community groups. They are essentially all the same: a group of like-minded believers coming together to be edified in truth and

The Invitation

community. Each time I step into the role of leading a new group, I'm struck by the beautiful diversity of the women who choose to show up. It's in the mix of personalities, perspectives, and stages of life that I'm reminded of the beauty of the body of Christ, that all are invited and welcome. Like 1 Corinthians 12:12 says, "The human body has many parts, but the many parts make up the whole body. So it is with the body of Christ" (NLT). No matter where someone is on their faith journey, no matter how messy life feels, there's a seat for everyone at the table. And it's often in that sacred, messy togetherness that the most powerful growth and connection happen.

Years ago I helped start a new discipleship group with a handful of women who didn't yet know each other. This is my favorite way to build community: bringing together women from different walks of life and watching genuine relationships form from the ground up. As we were building the group, our community pastor asked me to reach out to a new girl, Emma, to see whether she might be a good fit. Without hesitation I set up a coffee date, eager to extend an invitation and make her feel welcome.

When Emma arrived she was quiet and reserved, barely making eye contact. She seemed unsure, almost as if she were deciding whether she even wanted to be there. The conversation felt slow and hesitant, but I kept sharing about the group—how we were all figuring life out together, how no one had to show up perfect or polished. After an hour of conversation, I gave her the details of our next meeting and told her we'd love to see her there, hoping she felt even a small tug to step into the community waiting for her.

The Intentional Invitation

And that was that.

Emma didn't come. Week after week, she never showed up and never returned a text message. I had been ghosted. Toward the end of the semester, I felt the Lord prompting me to reach out to her again. We grabbed dinner this time—and we connected. I sat down with her and listened as she shared about her life. I didn't pressure her into coming to our group; I simply showed up and listened. As we wrapped up dinner and paid the bill, I told her about the group again and said we'd love for her to come.

That next week, she came. Emma had needed an intentional invitation. In fact, she needed several. If we are honest, isn't that how we feel sometimes? It can be hard for some to accept the first invitation, especially to something new, but the Lord doesn't want us to give up asking. He wants us to continue to extend the invitation. "Let us not become weary in doing good, for at the proper time we will reap a harvest if we do not give up. Therefore, as we have opportunity, let us do good to all people, especially to those who belong to the family of believers" (Gal. 6:9–10).

I never grew weary in inviting Emma, and over the next two years I witnessed her grow spiritually and emotionally. She went from being shy and intimidated to sharing her testimony of God's goodness in her own life. She invited others to experience what she had, all because she accepted the invitation.

The gospel is an invitation to come just as you are and enjoy a relationship with God: "All those the Father gives me will come to me, and whoever comes to me I will never drive away" (John 6:37). Therefore, the invitation to our table should be an extension of the gospel. It should act as the open door to sharing the gospel, to witnessing the goodness of God, and to sitting at the table with Jesus.

The invitation is simple; it's the gospel in action.

A Way of Life

Unlike the Martha Stewart version of hospitality, Christian hospitality isn't a special occasion or a performative event; it's a way of life. When you are an athlete, you don't just practice one time. You practice every day. If you want to hone your expertise in playing an instrument, you don't pick it up once and become a virtuoso. You must practice that instrument daily. When Paul wrote that we must practice hospitality, he wasn't referring to just men or just women. He wasn't saying that in certain stages of life we should practice hospitality. And he didn't single out those with the gift of hospitality. Instead, he stated to us all that hospitality should be a way of life, that it should be regularly honed and crafted.

Therefore, we need to be intentional about extending invitations. Hospitality doesn't happen by accident, and one of the defining marks of biblical hospitality is a willingness to invite others in, even when they may never return the gesture. As followers of Christ, we're called to open our tables to everyone, longing for each person to encounter the grace and love found in the gospel. As Jesus instructed us, "When you give a luncheon or dinner, do not invite your friends, your brothers or sisters, your

The Intentional Invitation

relatives, or your rich neighbors; if you do, they may invite you back and so you will be repaid. But when you give a banquet, invite the poor, the crippled, the lame, the blind, and you will be blessed" (Luke 14:12–14). When we invite those who Jesus has called us to, we can anticipate deep fellowship and authentic conversation that draw us closer to Jesus.

How can we effectively extend the invitation? What does it truly mean to invite someone to experience biblical hospitality? The beautiful truth is that it can take any form we choose. A glance through the Bible reveals diverse examples—sharing a meal in a tent (glamping anyone?) or enjoying a picnic on a hillside. I've brainstormed some genuine ways to extend this invitation, moving beyond the mere obligation to a more personal experience that reflects Jesus' heart for hospitality. As you read this list, be thinking about how you can intentionally invite others into your life in a way that reflects how Jesus did it throughout his ministry.

- **Make it personal.** Instead of sending a group text, consider reaching out to each person individually with a call or a personal message. Share the reasons you'd love for them to join you; this adds a thoughtful touch to the invitation. You might opt for a FaceTime or a voicemail. A video message, like those you can send on Marco Polo, can really elevate the invitation and make it feel even more special.
- **Invite a mix of guests.** Bringing together people from different backgrounds can enrich any experience. I

The Invitation

had the chance to do this for my thirtieth birthday, and it turned out to be a ton of fun. I invited six of my closest friends on a weeklong trip, and I had such a blast watching my friends get to know one another better and create wonderful memories. Not only was it a special time for me, but my friends ended up with new connections, each gaining five new friends. It was heartwarming to see how those friendships blossomed—a beautiful reminder of how powerful it can be to bring people together.

- **Use humor.** Lighten the invitation with humor. Send a funny meme or GIF that says, "My table has an empty chair with your name on it!" A little humor can break the ice and make the invitation feel friendly and relaxed.
- **Surprise invite.** I am queen of the spontaneous invite, and I think people love it. Surprise someone with an invitation for something spontaneous, like a last-minute dinner, coffee, or walk. Sometimes the best experiences are unplanned.
- **Make it a bring-a-friend event.** If you know someone who might feel more comfortable in a group setting, why not encourage them to bring a friend along? Having someone they know nearby can help ease any nervousness and make the experience more enjoyable. It's a wonderful way to share the adventure together. Plus, it creates an opportunity for both of them to make new friends.
- **Make it a theme.** Hosting themed gatherings can bring an extra layer of fun and excitement to your

The Intentional Invitation

get-togethers. Picture a cozy soup night during the winter months, where you and your friends can savor warm bowls of your favorite soups, trying and sharing recipes. A simple theme not only adds a festive touch but also turns a basic meetup into something special.

- **Include children or pets.** Before I became a mom, I never realized how hard it was to go to things when you have a child; including comments and bylines like "we are baby friendly" or "children welcome" are very appreciated. Go out of your way to make the invitation family friendly by encouraging people to bring their kids or pets. It makes your invitation inclusive and shows that you welcome your guests as they are.
- **Ordinary days.** Invite someone over for something as simple as "a Tuesday dinner" or a "laundry-folding night." This reminds people that hospitality isn't about the plan but about sharing everyday life together.

I recently watched an influencer on Instagram preparing for a costume party, and she invited her friend over to help with her makeup. I found it fascinating! As a DIY enthusiast, I pride myself on being independent and rarely asking for assistance. It never occurred to me to invite someone to do my makeup, because I usually handle it myself. However, after watching her Instagram Story, I realized I've been missing out. There's so much value in the camaraderie and memories that come from reaching out to others. Don't miss out on all that and the friendship formed by extending

The Invitation

an invitation and allowing someone to walk alongside you every day.

No matter what the invitation looks like—whether it's a simple coffee date, an invitation to share a meal, or a walk through your neighborhood—it's vital that we extend it, and even more so, that we make a practice of inviting people into our lives. Practicing biblical hospitality helps us grow and stretch our hearts to care for others as Jesus would. Each invitation is an opportunity to prioritize relationships, deepen our faith, and offer ourselves as vessels of God's love—even in the midst of life's busyness and chaos. In a world where so many feel unseen or disconnected, our invitations have the power to show others a glimpse of God's love and invite them into a place of belonging.

Back in the early church, Christians were known—they were actually famous—for their hospitality. During the plague in Alexandria in the 1300s, when everyone else left to escape the disease, it was the Christians who were known to stay and tend to the sick and dying.[1] They provided food, water, and shelter to those who needed it most; they displayed selfless hospitality to those Jesus would call "the least of these":

> "'For I was hungry and you gave me food, I was thirsty and you gave me drink, I was a stranger and you welcomed me, I was naked and you clothed me, I was sick and you visited me, I was in prison and you came to me.' Then the righteous will answer him saying, 'Lord, when did we see you hungry and feed you, or thirsty and give you drink?

The Intentional Invitation

And when did we see you a stranger and welcome you, or naked and clothe you? And when did we see you sick or in prison and visit you?' And the King will answer them, 'Truly, I say to you, as you did it to one of the least of these my brothers, you did it to me.'" (Matt. 25:35–40 ESV)

Are we famous for our hospitality? Is the church famous for the way we invite people in? Do we exist to make Jesus' name known through welcoming people to our table? What are we inviting people into?

Think about an invitation you've received. You might think about a physical invitation to a wedding or a party, one with postage that is addressed in swirly calligraphy. Maybe it's a regular out-of-the-blue text message from a friend inviting you over for dinner. Or, and this is my favorite, it's an invitation to do life with someone that comes out of a spontaneous conversation ordained by the Holy Spirit. You know, the kind of conversation where one thing leads to another, and suddenly you're sitting on their couch eating brownies and ice cream? That invitation is my favorite because there is no pomp and circumstance about it. It's extended from our love for connection and community.

Our Christian motivation for extending hospitality comes from our experience receiving hospitality from God. We did not deserve God or his invitation, and in fact, thanks to our sinful nature, we were separated from him. "But God demonstrates his own love for us in this: While we were still sinners, Christ died for us" (Rom. 5:8). That is the hospitality we receive from God, and whether you recognize it or not, hospitality is at the very center of understanding who God is. There is nothing we can do to reciprocate that type of love, and still he invited us into his house to sit at his table as his sons and daughters.

Where to Start

As we develop the habit of inviting others in, it can be easy to start with what feels like the most controllable piece: the food. But remember, it's not about the food; it's about the people. When people step into our environment, our job is to put Jesus' love on display, not to have a four-layer homemade strawberry cake with fresh mint from the backyard.

When it comes to inviting people over, it's all about creating a warm and welcoming atmosphere. You don't have to worry about formalities like addressed invitations or elaborate meals. Hospitality should be simple, uplifting, and life-giving. Start small and take it one step at a time. I've put together some questions to consider before inviting others over; these are questions I still think about. I can even remember jotting down my answers in my journal. It's just a small step, but it can help make hospitality a habit in our lives.

I. Who do you feel a tug in your heart to invite?

Pay attention to any specific individual who comes to mind. This recurring thought might be more than a coincidence; it could be a gentle nudge from the Holy Spirit encouraging you to reach out. Sometimes these reminders are God's way of highlighting someone who may need your kindness or support.

Take a moment to reflect on why this person stands out to you. Perhaps they're going through a challenging time, or maybe they're just looking for a friend or a listening ear. Whatever the reason, jotting down their name could be an important step in acknowledging this prompting and acting on it.

By noting their name somewhere accessible, you not only validate your intuition but also set the intention to reach out later. This small act can be incredibly powerful, serving as a reminder to check in on them or extend an invitation—whether for coffee, a chat, or even a deeper discussion about faith. Your willingness to listen and be present might make a significant difference in their life.

Take the nudge seriously and be open to what unfolds. You never know how a simple invitation could lead to meaningful connections or transformative conversations.

2. Where are you going to invite them?

Merriam-Webster defines *invitation* as "an often formal request to be present or participate."[2] We can't invite someone to something if we don't have a destination. Whether it's to a party or just to our home, there is always a destination for that invitation.

It's important to think through what you want the experience to be for you and your guest. Maybe it's not feasible for you to invite someone into your home, so instead you meet for lunch after the church service on Sunday. Let me

The Invitation

add a caveat and say that the distraction in a restaurant is much different from the distractions in your home. There is a foundational intimacy that comes from inviting someone into where you live, and vulnerability is naturally introduced into the conversation when you are in the comfort and seclusion of your own home. Just like you wouldn't try to have your quiet time in the middle of a football stadium, it's hard to have open and honest conversation in a public place. Remember, every invitation we extend to people to join us around our table is also an invitation to experience Jesus. So we want to find a place that is conducive to doing just that.

3. What are conversation topics you can prepare ahead of their arrival?

Is the person you invited going through something that you are aware of? Did they just move to the area? Or is the only thing you have in common with them that your children are in the same classroom? Think about planning conversation the way you would plan a recipe. If you want to make a crème brûlée, you don't just turn on the oven and begin cracking eggs. You want to make sure you have the ingredients, the tools, and the time to make the recipe first.

In the same way, we want to make sure we are prepared spiritually and mentally to invite others into our space. Invite God into the conversation and ask him to bless each word. Write out two or three topics and then pray over them that God would ordain the conversation. Just like he directs the words of pastors on Sunday mornings, we want to invite him to direct the time we have with our guests around our table.

4. How are you going to follow up with those you invite?

Staying in touch with new friends after inviting them into your home is key to building those relationships. A thoughtful follow-up shows that you truly appreciated the time spent together and are committed to keeping that connection alive. One of the simplest yet most meaningful ways to do this is by sending a handwritten note. In my family we call these a "happy," an unexpected treat that's given to show someone you were thinking about them. Receiving a letter in the mail is such a "happy," especially when I wasn't anticipating it and the other letters I find in the mail usually have to do with boring responsibilities. Handwritten notes demonstrate genuine care and show that you took the time to craft a thoughtful message. A brief note expressing how much you enjoyed someone's company or recalling a specific moment can leave a great impression. In today's world of digital communication, taking the time to write and mail a note adds a personal touch that conveys your hospitality. This little act of intentionality shows you've been reflecting on your time together and are genuinely interested in growing the friendship, making future gatherings even more special.

Sometimes, writing a handwritten note just doesn't happen, and that's okay. If putting pen to paper feels overwhelming, don't stress about it. What really matters is making the effort to follow up and being intentional with your response. A quick text is a simple and convenient way

The Invitation

to stay connected and suggest another hangout. Something like "I had such a fantastic time hosting you the other night! Let's plan to get together again soon!" keeps the fun going while feeling relaxed.

Often the conversations from your get-togethers can easily lead to another plan—whether it's a movie night, grabbing coffee, or just having a phone chat to continue building those relationships after being together. Reaching back out to others shows that they matter to you and adds a richness and depth to your friendship. What's even more beautiful is how these follow-up moments can blossom into deeper relationships, revealing unexpected blessings. A casual chat can turn into a trusted friendship, reminding us that every conversation holds the potential to enrich our lives in ways we never anticipated.

By actively pursuing these friendships, you're not just making connections; you're sharing love in a way that really resonates with others and helps strengthen those bonds. Trust that you'll find your way through this process, and with your sincere efforts, you can build relationships that honor something truly special and leave a lasting impact.

As you get acquainted with these questions, it might take practice for your responses to come quickly or for you to have these questions memorized. Don't worry if it doesn't happen overnight—extending hospitality in a genuine and authentic way takes practice. Just like you have resources to refer back to when you learn an instrument or begin learning a new hobby, consider bookmarking the next page and using these questions as a resource to your

The Intentional Invitation

journey of habit-forming hospitality, scribbling thoughts in the margins, or even keeping a journal to reflect on the invitations you have extended. Because each open door has the potential to reflect God's grace and help people experience him in new and intimate ways.

1. Who do you feel a tug in your heart to invite?
   _____

2. Where are you going to invite them?
   _____

3. What are conversation topics you can prepare ahead of their arrival?
   _____

4. How are you going to follow up with those you invite?
   _____

Now that you know who you are going to invite, where you are spending time with them, and what you can talk about, review the following invitational inventory I created as a tool to help you check your heart and prepare yourself for hospitality. By walking through these questions, you can thoughtfully assess your readiness to extend an invitation to others, cultivating a spirit of openness and generosity. Being honest in your responses will guide you in understanding what may hold you back, and it will help you focus on the intentional steps needed to make each invitation genuine

The Invitation

and welcoming. After reflecting, bookmark the inventory or take a photo of it to help you the next time the Spirit nudges you to reach out to someone in an authentic and intentional way.

INVITATIONAL INVENTORY

1. Do you find it easy to extend hospitality, even when it's inconvenient?
2. Do you often feel overwhelmed by the idea of hosting guests?
3. Do you feel like you're too busy to extend hospitality?
4. Are you comfortable inviting people who are different from you into your home?
5. Do you struggle to trust the Holy Spirit's promptings to invite others into your home?
6. Do you view hospitality as a directive from God, like the Great Commission, calling you to invite others in regardless of your personal feelings or inadequacies?
7. Do you believe hospitality can deepen your relationship with God?
8. Do you trust that the Holy Spirit wouldn't prompt you to offer hospitality unless he was ready to use you?
9. Do you feel the need to have a perfect home before inviting others over?

10. Are you actively cultivating a habit of hospitality in your life?
11. What causes you to hesitate when it comes to extending hospitality?
12. What typically holds you back from inviting others over?
13. What is the first thing you can do to start creating a habit of hospitality in your life?
14. Do you believe hospitality is a spiritual discipline you're called to practice?
15. What is the first step you can take to make hospitality a priority in your life?
16. Do you see hospitality as a form of service to God?
17. Do you find it difficult to let go of control when hosting guests?
18. Do you believe hospitality can bring joy and fulfillment to your life?
19. Do you often feel like you're not good enough to invite people in?
20. Do you believe hospitality can play a role in building your community?
21. Do you see hospitality as a form of spiritual growth?
22. How can welcoming people into your home help you practice the spiritual discipline of hospitality daily?
23. How can practicing hospitality help you cultivate a deeper relationship with the Holy Spirit?
24. If you were to pray for his help, do you believe the Holy Spirit could prompt you to invite specific people into your home?

The Invitation

25. How does prayer influence your ability to seek the Holy Spirit's guidance in practicing hospitality?
26. Does being an extrovert make hospitality feel less challenging for you or being an introvert make it more challenging?
27. Does hospitality seem overwhelming, or can small, practical steps help you experience the blessing of inviting people in and sharing Jesus with them?
28. Think back to a time you opened your door to someone. Did something sacred or surprising happen in the simplicity of that moment?
29. Do you see hospitality as more than just providing physical comforts but as creating a welcoming and inclusive atmosphere?
30. Do you believe your ability to be hospitable is based on personal merits and qualifications or something deeper?

The goal of this inventory is simple: to prepare your heart to invite others into your life and your home. This is more than just inviting someone to a meal; it's about opening a door to friendship, to hope, and to the love and truth of the gospel of Jesus. Let's set the table together, inviting those on the outside to take a seat. In doing so, you extend not only hospitality but also the joy of community and the blessing of feeling valued, seen, and known through an intentional invitation.

Chapter 8

• • • • •

Habitual Hospitality

As you begin incorporating hospitality into your daily life, you might reach a moment when everything starts to click. After hosting countless gatherings, sharing heartfelt conversations, and navigating a few hiccups along the way, you've finally gotten the hang of inviting people into your home and your life. But what happens next?

Once you really grasp the heart of biblical hospitality, you'll find that inviting others over becomes so much more than just a simple gathering. It's a beautiful practice that reflects God's love for us and invites us to participate in his work. As we open our doors and hearts, we create space for divine encounters and connections that reveal God's character. When we live out hospitality, we not only showcase his love but also inspire others to do the same. When

The Invitation

you finally get to the other side of creating the rhythm of hospitality in your life, you'll look back and see the closeness you've cultivated with God, recognizing the profound difference that serving and loving others through his eyes makes. This journey isn't just about being a good host; it's about spiritual transformation that changes how you experience God's love and grace.

In the last chapter we focused on the importance of the invitation—how it opens the door for connection, how it draws people in, and how we can practice the art of hospitality by extending that invitation. But there's a deeper level to hospitality that goes beyond the moment of inviting someone into our home. Once you feel comfortable inviting others in and it becomes second nature, you'll begin to notice a subtle shift in your mindset, a shift that opens your eyes to new opportunities for outreach, ministry, and even deeper connection. It's as though hospitality transforms from a simple act into a ministry of service, showing love not just in the tangible things we offer but in the invitation itself.

The reality is, as you practice hospitality, you start to see its potential as an ongoing rhythm in your life. The more you extend an invitation, the more you begin to notice its ripple effect—the way it invites others into your life, the way it brings the community around you closer together, and the way it draws you nearer to God. You begin to recognize that hospitality is not just a task; it's a habit. And when something becomes a habit, it becomes a part of who you are.

A. W. Tozer captures the sentiment of holy habits: "[God] knows that we have set the direction of our hearts toward Jesus, and we can know it too, and comfort ourselves with the knowledge that a habit of soul is forming which will become after a while a sort of spiritual reflex requiring no more conscious effort on our part."[1] When we commit to a lifetime of habitual hospitality, we are chasing after a deeper intimacy with God.

According to a study conducted at Duke University, habits account for about 40 percent of our behaviors on any given day.[2] These behaviors, whether intentional or not, are powerful. This is why it's important to be intentional about what we allow to become habitual. Proverbs cautions, "Above all else, guard your heart, for everything you do flows from it" (4:23) and "Be wise, and set your heart on the right path" (23:19). The authors of Proverbs knew the benefits and consequences of our habits compound over time, and they shape who we are.

You might already have solid habits in your health, household chores, or work, but what about your habits when it comes to Jesus? Let's call them holy habits. A holy habit is just a fun term for a spiritual discipline—anything that draws us closer to God through the process of sanctification. Holy habits require us to dedicate our time to developing them, and the habit of hospitality is no different. When we make hospitality a rhythm in our lives, it becomes a way of living out our faith and serving others. It's not just an invitation; it's an opportunity for ministry. And as you begin to embrace this habit, you'll soon realize that hospitality is not just about having people over. It's about cultivating a purpose, a calling, a ministry of inviting others into the grace and peace of God's love.

Hospitality feels harder than ever—and not because we

The Invitation

lack tools to make life easier but because we're busier than ever. It's wild when you think about it. We have apps, automation, and AI designed to save us time, yet our calendars have never been more crammed. If you are anything like me, it's not unusual to be double- or triple-booked on any given day.

The list of responsibilities we have is so overwhelming that by the time we get to spending quiet time with Jesus, reading Scripture, or opening our homes to others for hospitality, it seems impossible to focus or do each task meaningfully. We run ourselves ragged just trying to keep up with everything. So when we invite someone over and want to be hospitable, it's important for us to slow down and be intentional.

Several years ago my sister Molly Anne had young children and was starting her own photography business. With a toddler and infant twins at home, she was finding it nearly impossible to keep her house picked up. By 10 a.m. her home looked like a tornado had swept through. In the middle of her busy schedule, between nursing and working, she decided to practice a new behavior that would develop into a habit over time: the ten-minute timer. It's a focused tidy-up to make your space feel more presentable in just ten minutes by picking up clutter and wiping down surfaces. However, she didn't feel like she had even ten minutes, so she shortened it to five minutes. She was amazed at what she could accomplish in that short amount of time. It wasn't about putting everything away or having a spotless house, but it was about creating the habit of setting aside time to check just a few things off her chore list.

Habitual Hospitality

In this same way, we can create habits through taking small steps. But before we create habits, we must recognize the need for them in our lives. If Molly Anne hadn't recognized that her home carried an undercurrent of chaos by 10 a.m., she might not have seen the need for change. But once she did she leaned into a new habit—a habit that brought a surprising sense of calm and clarity to her day and family. As it began to shape her days, she shared the simple shift with some friends and family. Before long, others were trying it, too, and finding that it made a difference in their lives as well.

To create a lifelong habit of hospitality, we will need to rethink our priorities. For some it might feel like we need to add an extra five hours to each day. But you don't need five extra hours; you just need to take one small transforming step. When hospitality becomes a regular practice, it can profoundly affect how you invite others into your life. This consistency allows you to cultivate deeper relationships, as inviting others over becomes less about the logistics of hosting and more about sharing your life.

As you establish hospitality as a lifelong habit, you may find that it transforms from a one-time event into a lifestyle rooted in love, openness, and community. Regularly inviting people into your life fosters an atmosphere of trust and vulnerability, creating a safe space for authentic conversations and shared experiences. Over time these interactions can open your heart and home in ways you never anticipated as others recognize your home as a place where they are truly seen and appreciated. This ripple effect can inspire others to embrace hospitality in their own lives, creating a network of encouragement and love.

The Invitation

When you invite people into your life, you reflect God's welcoming nature and his desire for us to live in community. As you make hospitality a priority, you become more attuned to the needs of those around you, whether it's offering a listening ear, a warm meal, or simply a comforting presence. This awareness enriches your life and the lives of those you invite in, transforming every moment into an opportunity for growth, healing, and connection.

Unfortunately, hospitality won't ever become a habit in our lives until we give it the attention it deserves and view it as a way to connect not only with others but also more intimately with Jesus. A life of hospitality begins in worship with a recognition of God's own hospitality—his generosity and his welcome. We will begin to make a habit out of hospitality when we remember how much Jesus is present in the habit of welcoming others in. While hospitality was a significant practice in generations past, it has been lost in our culture today, making it even harder and all the more important to reconnect ourselves with this habit day in and day out.

For those with the gift of hospitality, it looks easy and enjoyable; it's as second nature as breathing. But for others—really, most of us—the habit must be cultivated. True hospitality isn't just about opening our homes; it's about opening our hearts to a holy habit of welcoming others, embracing differences, and continually stretching ourselves to make room for people in our lives. The beauty of hospitality is that the more we practice it, the more natural it becomes, and over time it shapes not only how we care for others but how we reflect God's glory in our interactions with others.

When we start to train our minds to think about things

differently, as Molly Anne did, we will begin to see the benefit of forming whatever habit we are trying to create. We set goals for ourselves, and those goals help us measure our accomplishments. However, goals get us nowhere without habits in place to achieve them. Just like Molly Anne's goal of the five-minute sweep, the goal for any holy habit is to form a desire that, through obedience, produces godly character. Our habits produce a spiritual transformation that leads us to a deeper understanding of who God is and his desires for us.

In the Sermon on the Mount (Matt. 5–7), Jesus spoke of the process of spiritual transformation. The Pharisees and teachers were obsessed with the laws of the land and less concerned with issues of the heart. But Jesus taught us that it's not the outward appearance of the person that matters but his inward intentions. He said, "Blessed are the pure in heart, for they shall see God" (Matt. 5:8 ESV). Our habits are a direct reflection of the discipline in our hearts and minds.

By embracing hospitality as a means to grow spiritually, you're not just welcoming others every now and then; you're also opening yourself up to transformation, allowing God to work through your relationships and experiences to draw you closer to him. You can do this—if you are willing to practice. As apprentices of Jesus, you and I have both the ability and the responsibility to set our minds on him.

Habit Forming

I love a good process. I like a plan with purpose. My family jokes that every night before bed my famous last words are,

The Invitation

"What's your plan tomorrow?" I'm sure they will find a way to put that on my epitaph. I thrive with a plan. I think plans are biblical; without proper processes in place, our goal of forming good habits will surely fail.

Look at Abraham: God made a promise to him, a covenant that would extend to his descendants. Later when the Israelites were preparing to enter the land God had set aside for them, he gave them the law to guide their lives and draw them back to him. And ultimately, God sent Jesus to be our perfect example, showing us how to live in such a way that we reflect his character and show his love. He always had a plan to equip his people with good habits. Because we don't serve a chaotic God; we serve one who loves order and is preparing his people for what's ahead.

Andy Crouch, a Christian author and journalist, speaks about the practices and rhythms of Christian living, calling these "A Rule of Life," and he says that we need to have a "set of practices to guard our habits and guide our lives."[3] Crouch was writing for entrepreneurs when he first introduced this idea, but I think it can be applied as we pursue holy habits. So let's take what we've learned about the spiritual discipline of hospitality and create a plan to live a life marked by serving others.

Below I've identified a few examples of how you can create microhabits that will multiply to produce macroresults in your journey to developing hospitality as a habit. These are little triggers I've set up to remind me to practice hospitality. Without them I might rely only on what I call my Big 4—Friendsgiving, Christmas, the Super Bowl, and Galentine's Day—to be my reminders to practice hospitality

Habitual Hospitality

throughout the year. Instead, I choose to use these seemingly insignificant triggers to prompt me to always keep hospitality and extending the welcome at the top of my mind.

OPEN-DOOR POLICY

"Always be prepared to give an answer to everyone who asks you to give the reason for the hope that you have." (I Peter 3:15)

My Why
I want my friends to know they can come over at any time and feel confident that I will welcome them with open arms.

The Process
My nonnegotiables are the tasks I do every evening before I go to bed or every morning before I leave the house. Then if I see anyone during my day, I can feel confident that my house is ready for guests.

Remember, your house will not be perfect; that's not the goal. The goal is to feel comfortable extending the welcome to whomever the Spirit puts on your heart, whenever he puts it on your heart.

This list might not contain your nonnegotiables, but I bet you have your own things that need to be done. As an example, here are my mine:

1. Bed made
2. Sink clean
3. Pillows on the couch (not the floor)

The Invitation

BIRTHDAY SURPRISES

"Love one another with brotherly affection. Outdo one another in showing honor." (Rom. 12:10 ESV)

My Why
Intentionality is so important to cultivating community. Birthdays are an easy opportunity to help someone feel loved, valued, and seen.

The Process
When the Spirit places people in my life to pursue and love with hospitality, their birthday goes on my calendar. The week of their birthday, I'll pick up cookies, brownie mix, or a small bouquet from the grocery store. Then, by inviting my friend over—or inviting myself over to their home—I'm able to spend time with them, show them love, and help them feel valued during a special time.

A LITTLE HAPPY

"Now that you have purified yourselves by obeying the truth so that you have sincere love for each other, love one another deeply, from the heart." (1 Peter 1:22)

My Why
In my pursuit of living a life marked by hospitality, I want to cultivate a heart that cares profoundly for others. Little happies remind me to put others first and practice that sacrificial hospitality that Peter commanded us to.

Habitual Hospitality

The Process

Remember when I mentioned my family's habit of bringing a "happy" to someone? Well, I've taken this concept and put my own hospitality spin on it! A little happy is a monthly commitment to intentionally practice hospitality for a specific person. By showing up for this chosen person at least three times during that month, I'm making a conscious effort to be the hands and feet of Jesus and put the gospel on display. This rhythm has the opportunity to have profound impact on someone's life and is a small way to be obedient and foster a sense of connection and community. Here are a couple of examples of how I've been practicing this recently:

1. A friend's mother had surgery and was staying with my friend, so I sent them a little happy that included sweet treats and candles to help take some of the burden off.
2. My favorite little happy is to invite new mothers from church over. We meet while dropping our children off in their Sunday school classroom, and then a friendship blooms from there.

COFFEE OF THE MONTH

"Don't forget to show hospitality to strangers, for some who have done this have entertained angels without realizing it!" (Heb. 13:2 NLT)

My Why

There are people I don't know who need community, who are searching for connection with other believers. Knowing

The Invitation

this helps me stay focused on regularly inviting outsiders into intimate community.

The Process

Coffee of the Month is a fantastic way to foster community and connection. By inviting people over once a month for coffee and conversation, I'm creating a welcoming and inclusive space for individuals to share what's going on in their lives, experience Jesus in an authentic way, and build meaningful relationships. It's a simple yet powerful way to bring people together and make outsiders feel like insiders.

THE SIX-MONTH MARATHON

"I'm here inviting outsiders, not insiders—an invitation to a changed life, changed inside and out." (Luke 5:32 MSG)

My Why

We all know about Friendsgiving and Christmas parties; they are a great gateway to hospitality. Did you know there is a six-month marathon of hospitality moments after New Year's? We can use these celebrations to practice hospitality, invite outsiders in, and create a welcoming environment to love on those who might not know Christ.

The Process

The six-month marathon includes the Super Bowl, Galentine's Day, St. Patrick's Day, Easter, Cinco de Mayo, and the Fourth of July.

Habitual Hospitality

By opening my home and inviting people to gather around different smaller holidays, I can create a festive and inviting atmosphere that encourages community.

While many may be hesitant to attend a church service or come to a prayer meeting, they may be more inclined to join a social event at your home. This provides a more casual and comfortable setting for people to connect and for you to put God's love on display.

As we embrace these practices, we begin to weave hospitality into the very fabric of our lives, transforming not only our relationships with others but also deepening our walk with God. When we intentionally cultivate a lifestyle of habitual hospitality, we allow God's love to flow through us in tangible ways. Each invitation becomes an opportunity to reflect his grace and warmth, turning our homes into sanctuaries of connection and compassion. These microhabits serve as spiritual anchors, reminding us that hospitality is more than just an action or a one-off invitation to someone in our periphery; it's a reflection of our relationship with Christ and a way to demonstrate his love to the world around us.

In committing to a life of habitual hospitality, we align ourselves with God's order and purpose, experiencing his transformative power in the process. As we practice these small acts of service, we not only build community but also grow in intimacy with our Creator. So let us be diligent in nurturing these habits, knowing that they will lead to a life enriched with love, grace, and a deeper

The Invitation

understanding of who God is. In this journey we discover that every invitation is a chance to encounter God's presence, creating a ripple effect of hospitality that echoes his heart in our world.

Part 3
The Transformation

Chapter 9

• • • • • •

The Great Invite

You could make the argument that one of Christianity's foundational principles is hospitality. Starting in Genesis, hospitality is laced throughout Abraham's story. God planned to establish a relationship with people through Abraham, and this relationship is characterized by an openness, a welcome, and an unconditional love. Later, Jesus, as the fulfillment of God's promise to Abraham, further embodies this spirit of hospitality.

Scripture is full of incredible examples of hospitality from leaders in the faith. The author of Hebrews reminded us, "Do not neglect to show hospitality to strangers, for thereby some have entertained angels unawares" (13:2 ESV). This verse points back to Abraham's story in Genesis 18:1–15, when he welcomed three unexpected visitors into his tent and

The Transformation

eagerly offered them a meal. I believe this is a direct call to action to embrace hospitality as a daily practice and to carry a heart posture of welcome. Abraham's hospitality became a sacred moment where God showed up and his promises unfolded: the promise that Abraham's wife, Sarah, would bear a son.

Just like Abraham welcomed unknown travelers into his home and insisted they stay for dinner, we, too, should always seek to create a space where people feel welcomed and fed—both physically and spiritually.

In God's eyes the idea of hospitality goes way beyond just sharing meals. It's a huge part of what it means to be a Christian. There is a theme throughout Scripture of treating the outsider like the insider, inviting them to feel included. Jesus wondered pretty plainly in the Gospel of Luke: "If you only love the lovable, do you expect a pat on the back?" (6:31–34 MSG). Eek!

It's easy to love those we enjoy being around and who give back to us. I would much rather extend an invitation to my closest friends to come over to my house than a stranger. However, that's not what God is asking us to do. He is asking us to invite the outsiders—those we aren't super close with and who might not think, speak, act, vote, or love like we do.

I love inviting people into my home, because for a brief period of time I get to love on someone without expecting anything in return. When I invite someone over for dinner, I don't expect that they will walk in with dessert or a bouquet of fresh flowers for the table. I invite them in to sit with me at my table as family. This offer is extended to outsiders, to treat them like they are in the inner circle.

The Great Invite

What does that really mean? To treat an outsider like an insider? Leviticus 19 says, "When a foreigner resides among you in your land, do not mistreat them. . . . Love them as yourself, for you were foreigners in Egypt" (vv. 33–34). The idea is carried throughout Deuteronomy when God is commanding the Israelites to love strangers because they used to be strangers in Egypt. Later in the Old Testament God's prophets remind the nations of Israel and Judah that God will judge them based on how they take care of strangers, orphans, and widows (Isa. 1:17; Jer. 22:3; Ezek. 22:7). In other words, how they treat outsiders will put their obedience to God on display for their community.

Is our hospitality so evident to others and centered around sharing Jesus that God's glory is on display and not our own?

Here's how I think about it: Inviting close family and friends over for Thanksgiving dinner isn't necessarily biblical hospitality. It's hospitable, but let's be honest, most people do that. Remember the verse "Do you expect a pat on the back?" (Luke 6:31–34 MSG)? As we continue thinking about what Scripture teaches us about hospitality, I want us to think deeper about what the invitation really looks like.

Let's pause and think about what an invitation means. On one side, it is something physical that welcomes someone into our space to feel loved, valued, and seen. On the other side, it is something spiritual that brings someone to experience Jesus at the table in a new, intimate, and authentic way. This is how Jesus did his ministry.

Jesus didn't have a home, a table, or a kitchen to invite others into, yet his invitation to fellowship was always

The Transformation

present. After his resurrection, Jesus met his disciples on the shore and prepared breakfast for them over a charcoal fire. He called out to them, "Come and have some breakfast!" (John 21:12 NLT). This simple meal was a powerful act of hospitality, not defined by wealth or status but by presence and love. Just like when he invited himself to Zacchaeus's house (Luke 19:5), Jesus' invitations were never about material things. They were about connection and restoration. His generosity flowed from a heart that offered living water, not from the possessions he had. If you feel like you can't extend hospitality because of what you lack, remember that true hospitality starts with a willingness to show up and create space for others. And if we're honest, many of the reasons we hesitate to invite others in are just excuses that keep us from experiencing the joy and connection God designed us for.

We aren't alone in feeling inadequate and creating excuses that keep us from experiencing the blessing God has for us in obeying him. In Scripture we see the disciples also came up with excuses. When five thousand people followed Jesus into the wilderness to listen to him teach (John 6:1–15), they got hungry—I mean, naturally, right? Sit anywhere long enough and someone will need a snack! The disciples didn't have any food to give five thousand people, so they wanted to tell them to go home. On one hand, they didn't have food, but on the other hand, I imagine the disciples were pretty hungry as well. But Jesus commanded them to go see if there was any food in the crowd.

The disciples came back and had enough food for maybe two people. In the midst of what I envision was their grumbling and complaining, Jesus turned what we see as inadequate into abundance. He could have just met the needs of his disciples that day. He could have fed only his crew. Instead, he miraculously multiplied the food so that it fed five thousand outsiders. He invited the outsiders to feel like insiders and to be fed not only physically but spiritually.

A few chapters back we talked about how preparation needs to become second nature. One person I imagine could be mentioned in this story is the mom (or family member) who packed the lunch for the little boy that day before he headed out of the house. She had no idea that her simple act of care, a habit formed out of love—making her son's lunch—would end up feeding five thousand people. That's the unseen power of obedience. We can't always know the impact of our hospitality, but our role isn't to measure the outcome. It's to faithfully extend the invitation. No matter how small or insignificant it may feel, our willingness to open our lives and invite others in could be the very thing God uses to meet someone's deepest need.

And deep down, we all want to be invited. We were designed by Christ to crave connection and community, and the invitation welcomes us into belonging. As we witness the early church being created throughout the New Testament, it serves as a great reminder that the church—the body of believers—made space for one another and modeled what it means to be the family of God.

As Paul traveled throughout his ministry, he wrote to the early churches and thanked the various people who showed him hospitality. He was encouraged and edified through their kindness. Fellowship within the body of Christ does

The Transformation

that. It lifts our spirits, reminds us we're not alone, and roots us in a family where love overflows. When we extend the invitation, we don't just bless others. We receive the blessing of hospitality: a shared life, where there is always a home, always a family, and always a place to belong.

Skip Heitzig said in one of his sermons, "Judaism and Christianity are singing religions. Atheism is songless, because they have nothing to sing about."[1] I think you could replace the word *singing* with *hospitable*: Christianity and Judaism are hospitable religions, because we have something (Someone) we want to invite you to experience. The invitation isn't reserved for the perfect or the put-together. It doesn't require you to fit a mold. Christianity is radically inclusive; the table is set, and *everyone* is invited to come and experience the love of Christ.

As Christians we're not just created for community. We're called to covenantal community. Lovable or unlovable, convenient or inconvenient, in celebration or in sorrow, we are commanded to show up for one another and "carry each other's burdens" (Gal. 6:2). Is there a better way to feel loved than to be welcomed into the beautifully messy, ordinary rhythms of someone's life? It is there, in the middle of life's ups and downs, that we have the joy of seeing how true gospel living manifests in the life of the Christ-follower. It is there that we learn how to pray for and love one another despite our differences.

So when you feel hesitant to extend an invitation, remember, hospitality isn't about perfection or performance. It's about the obedience in the invitation. It's about recognizing that someone somewhere is longing to be invited, and your simple yes to God could be the very answer to that longing.

To the Ends of Your Zip Code

A few weeks before John Maverick was born, Kyle and I moved into a new neighborhood. After his birth, as I camped out in the living room and nursed my son like it was my full-time job (because let's be honest, it was), I couldn't help but notice the endless parade of people walking their dogs. And trust me, I wasn't just window-gazing out of boredom. It was hard to miss the fact that everyone, and I mean everyone, paused to look at the giant stork sign we'd planted in the yard like a proud declaration to the world: "Yep, we made a human!"

While I nursed, Kyle was on dog-walking duty and met a lot of our neighbors. He'd always report back on who our new neighbors—dogs and humans—were with stories and interesting facts he'd learned. After almost five months of being cooped up in my house trying to figure out life with a newborn, I crawled out of my cave, pajamas and all, to meet one of the neighbors. Kyle had mentioned this neighbor was living alone for a few months while her husband was away at work, and I felt the nudge to rush outside and strike up a conversation. That conversation lasted longer than I had intended, but near the end I felt that small voice inside urging me to invite her inside to play with my baby. You could see her face light up as she accepted a rain check, and then she proceeded to share her phone number with me.

The Transformation

I can't tell you the end of that story because it's not over. She knocks on my front door somewhat frequently. One time I literally had dinner on the stove, and she just walked right in my front door and started sharing her life with me.

Friends, I want to encourage you to develop that type of hospitality. The kind that leaves the front door open for friends, old and new, to pop in and fill their soul with connection. I couldn't have extended the invitation that day had I not listened to the Spirit's prompting. I couldn't have listened to the Spirit had I not spent time with the Lord, preparing my heart and my space for someone to walk into. And I wouldn't have had my space ready to welcome someone in had I not been disciplined about creating the habit of hospitality in my life.

My neighbor doesn't offer anything. She doesn't bring fresh-baked pies or reciprocate the invitation. In fact, on the outside, it probably looks very one-sided. One thing I can tell you is that I am by far the primary beneficiary of this friendship. The blessing I receive from God through this random relationship between neighbors and the way I get to experience connection far outweigh anything my neighbor could bring.

I wonder if that is what Jesus thought as he prepared to die on the cross. I wonder if his death on the cross was his invitation to live in community with him for eternity, knowing full well that we could not bring anything to compare with his sacrifice.

I am by no means comparing our habit of hospitality to the sacrifice Jesus made and saying they are equal. Not in the slightest. But I am posing the question, What if the way we practice the spiritual discipline of hospitality gives us a glimpse of who God is?

What if, just by inviting someone in, they get to experience God in a whole new way? Would the invitation be worth it? Would the inconvenience or discomfort or self-doubt be worth it?

When we, as Christians, practice hospitality for the purpose of loving God and others, a natural by-product is the process of sanctification: the process by which we become more like Jesus. Creating community becomes second nature, and conversations organically bend toward reflecting Jesus and who he has called us to be. Jesus said, "Therefore go and make disciples of all nations, baptizing them in the name of the Father and of the Son and of the Holy Spirit" (Matt. 28:19). The call to go out and make disciples is not just for some people. I believe that your neighborhood, your community, and the groups you are involved in can and should be your mission field.

Yes, God calls some to the ends of the earth, but what if he called you to the ends of your zip code to bring those people to your table to experience him? Befriending our unbelieving neighbors, acquaintances, and coworkers in normal life situations can draw them to the glorious gospel in ways that a cold invitation to church from a stranger cannot. Inviting an unbeliever into your life gives them a front-row seat to see how the gospel changes regular, real, sinful people. What an opportunity to share the light of Christ with a dark world!

Yes, it's the Great Commission. But what if we rephrased it to the Great Invite?

The Transformation

This radical hospitality—the kind that reaches beyond comfort zones and genuinely welcomes people in—is at the heart of God's character. It's a simple yet powerful way to show others who he is. Paul's call for us to offer ourselves as living sacrifices, "holy and acceptable to God" (Rom. 12:1 ESV), can seem abstract at first. But what does it really mean to be a living sacrifice? It's not about laying down your life in the dramatic sense of martyrdom or becoming a full-time missionary. Instead, it's about making our everyday lives an offering to God. When Paul uses the term "living sacrifice," he's urging us to surrender our entire selves—our time, our relationships, our resources, and our actions—to serving God in tangible ways.

Think about how you spend your time. If you invite a neighbor over for coffee, you're not just socializing. You're offering that time to God by using it to build relationships, show love, and reflect his character. It's in the small, everyday choices where we lay down our personal preferences and make room for others that we truly live out this sacrifice. It's not always glamorous or grand, but it's deeply impactful. When Paul said this is "holy and acceptable to God," he meant that it's these ordinary, seemingly insignificant acts of kindness, generosity, and hospitality that honor God the most. They're the moments when we choose love over convenience, service over self-interest. By inviting others into our lives, we're not just practicing hospitality—we're living out our worship to a supreme God.

Hospitality is a theme throughout the stories in Scripture; we've discussed some of them already. If you have

The Great Invite

read any hospitality books, you can probably name the main stories: Abraham and the three visitors, Elisha and the Shunammite woman, Peter's mother-in-law, Mary and Martha, and Zacchaeus. But I want to take us somewhere else in Scripture—Sodom and Gomorrah.

In Genesis 18 God revealed to Abraham that intense judgment was coming to Sodom, where Abraham's nephew Lot lived. Verse 20 states that the sin of those who lived in Sodom was "very grave" (ESV). You've probably read this story before and know that Sodom struggled with sexual sin. But if you study Scripture beyond Genesis, you'll read that Ezekiel painted a bigger picture. Ezekiel 16:49 says that Sodom's grave sin was that they didn't help the poor and needy. I love how the New Living Translation version says it: "Sodom's sins were pride, gluttony, and laziness, while the poor and needy suffered outside her door." The city had an extreme, selfish devotion to what they wanted and desired, instead of supporting others in need. This kind of love becomes self-centered and excludes anyone on the outside.

Sodom wasn't hospitable; they let their pride trump their invitation. That was the point Ezekiel was making to the Israelites. He basically told them, "You are worse than Sodom. Your pride and idolatry have separated you from God, just like the inhospitableness of those in Sodom." This account reminds us that biblical hospitality is so much more than just being polite or setting out snacks.

When I read this story, I feel all sorts of things. First—can I be honest?—I've been there. I've been the one holding

The Transformation

all the invitations to the party and singling out the people I deemed "cool" by the world's standards. I have selfishly avoided the looks, the glances, and the gossip that ensues when I've invited the outsider.

The phrase "you can't sit with us" from the movie *Mean Girls* comes to my mind. I can actually hear Gretchen Wieners say it; the movie and scene are vivid in my mind. Watching that scene play out in real time, we think, *I would never act like that*. Yet many times we have withheld the invitation out of convenience, pride, and arrogance.

Second, on reading this story I find myself with a name on my mind and a tug on my heart to invite that person into my home this week. Do you? Who is the outsider in your sphere of influence that you need to extend an invitation to? That nudge you feel is the Holy Spirit. As we talked about earlier, the Holy Spirit will put a specific person or people on your heart to invite. Invite them.

Hospitality goes beyond just having a skill; it begins with a genuine disposition of love toward others, even strangers. To practice true hospitality, our hearts must be open and generous. Regardless of how skilled we are in cooking or homemaking, our guests can sense whether we possess this welcoming spirit. They perceive it in our gaze, our warmth, and our engagement. The key to increasing our capacity to extend this type of hospitality lies in experiencing the life-changing message of the gospel of Jesus Christ. Through this transformative experience, we cultivate the right attitude and heartfelt generosity needed to embrace outsiders and make them feel at home.

The Great Invite

Outsiders

The term *outsider* has been used frequently in this chapter, so I'd like to take a moment to define it. An outsider isn't just someone you've never met before. In this chapter I'm using the word in a slightly different way.

I have a saying with some of my closest friends: "You are my bullseye." Picture a bullseye with concentric circles. I've provided a visual representation so you can see exactly who the outsiders in your life are. If you're someone who likes to jot down notes in your books, write down the names of people in the different circles. The outsiders aren't the people within the target; they're the ones outside that target. They're not your friends, family, or community, but those who don't fit into any of those circles.

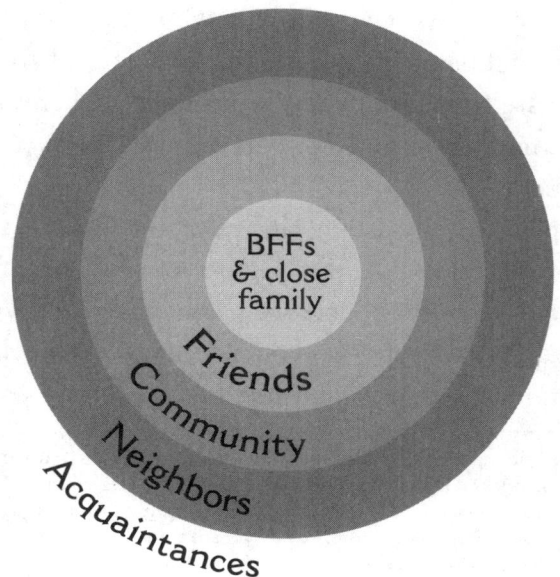

The Transformation

There is a girl who has been part of my social circle for the last few years, but I have never invited her over. I am outgoing and vivacious, while she is quiet, timid, and doesn't usually initiate conversations. However, during the few conversations we've had, she's had a lot to say, and I've felt the nudge of the Holy Spirit to invite her over several times. But I'm not sure what to say to an introvert. (I'm kidding!)

Truthfully the idea of hanging out with someone who is very different from me, who doesn't seem to want to talk much, and who I don't know well sounded like a daunting task. That's pride. That's arrogance. I dreaded the thought of showing hospitality to someone who wasn't on the inside of my bullseye, and my pride got in the way of experiencing Jesus more intimately.[*]

As we grow deeper in our understanding of the gospel, we will inevitably begin noticing who our neighbors are. Our eyes will be opened to see the outsiders all around us. Chances are there are people within your sphere of influence you have never noticed. You don't see them. You don't notice them.

Simply begin by asking this question: Who is the outsider in my world? Give this person your full attention; we pay attention to the people we value. Then ask, What do they need? What keeps them outside? How can I help? How can community impact their life?

---

[*] Update: I felt convicted writing those last few words. I invited her over, and guess what happened? She had a lot to say. In fact, she blessed me in more ways than I feel like I blessed her. She was so encouraging and had a contagious laugh that really brought a lot of joy to my day. We had a great time sitting around on my patio and drinking coffee; it was an easy afternoon.

The Great Invite

We offer hospitality in light of our expectations of eternity and in response to the gospel, not as a strategic way to get an immediate return on investment. Guests can usually discern if they are being offered fake or genuine hospitality. We can't fully experience love through hospitality if we aren't first genuinely honest or authentic in the invitation.

Friends, we're all so busy, and because it's much easier to do life without exposure to "the outsider," a strong expression of hospitality will not be automatic—we must be intentional about the invite. Unless there is a daily commitment, the habit won't form itself.

Meaningful hospitality, the kind where we invite others in without any expectation of reciprocation, is too important to be disregarded as a checkbox on our to-do list. So let's commit to the invite. Let's commit to prayerfully living out the gospel and rediscovering that hospitality is essential to our lives as Christians. And if our goal is to reflect God's glory and make his name known to the ends of the earth, then we must create a habit of hospitality by serving those both in and outside our circles.

Chapter 10

• • • • • •

Serving Others Without Burning Out

As you embark on this journey, I know it can feel daunting. The lists of things you need to do, the people you could invite, and the conversations you must initiate seem to keep growing. And you now must find the time to create the space in your otherwise-busy schedule to slow down and be intentional with your relationships.

This is when the Enemy will start to creep into your thoughts in the guise of burnout, often unnoticed until it feels overwhelming. Burnout is a type of exhaustion that stems not only from being busy but also from feeling stretched too thin—like a rubber band one snap away from breaking. I think we can all agree that with overcommitment, emotional and physical fatigue, and the chronic

The Transformation

busyness we find ourselves in, burnout is inevitable. And let's be honest: When you're running on empty, showing hospitality to others is nearly impossible.

Think about the last time you said yes to something because you felt like you *should*, not because you truly had the margin. Maybe it was signing up to bring snacks to the school event after a long workday or squeezing in one more coffee date even though your laundry pile was silently judging you from across the room. Over time, these small decisions add up, draining the joy and energy from the very things we long to do well.

Burnout has a sneaky way of making us resentful toward the opportunities for community and friendship that God desires us to embrace. Satan has a tendency to pervert the blessings God gives us, like the wonderful gift of hospitality, transforming them into a heavy burden that can feel exhausting and overwhelming. And this often leads to feeling lonely and frustrated. What was designed to bring joy and connection can, if we're not careful, become a source of stress and distraction, pulling our focus away from the ones God has called us to love.

Here's the message I want you to hear clearly in this chapter: On the journey to creating a life filled with hospitality, we must establish boundaries to avoid burnout. This means balancing a life of welcoming others with intentional emotional and physical limits that allow for personal time with God. By doing so, we create space for him to replenish our hearts, enabling us to pour into others from a place of peace rather than exhaustion. When we release ourselves from the unrealistic expectations that lead to burnout, we create space for the kind of hospitality that nourishes both us and the people we welcome.

If you've been living the lonely, isolated, overwhelming, and demanding life that comes from a culture scheduling us from the time we wake up to the time we lie down, you're not alone. I've been there. The encouragement I've found is that the gospel has freedom built into the pure essence of what we believe. It tells us that we can throw off the pressures that our culture is putting on us, and we can focus on the process of sanctification. Reread that. Exhale.

Do you feel a sense of relief? Was a burden just lifted off your shoulders?

I love the way Allie Beth Stuckey puts it: "We're not enough—period. And that's okay, because God is. The answer to our insufficiency and insecurity isn't self-love, but God's love. In Jesus, we're offered a way out of our toxic culture of self-love and into a joyful life of relying on him for wisdom, satisfaction, and purpose."[1] Here's the thing about self-love: It's become a buzzword. Our culture and social media have become obsessed with the notion that we must put ourselves first. They've defined this term not in stewarding our view of ourselves and valuing ourselves through God's eyes as his creation but in viewing ourselves with a selfish me-first attitude. True self-love doesn't internally idolize; it actually honors God. When Jesus said in Mark 12:31, "Love your neighbor as yourself," he didn't imply self-centeredness. Rather he pointed to a balanced, God-focused love—one where caring for ourselves allows us to serve others better. Self-love becomes meaningful when it flows from understanding our identity in Christ.

The Transformation

When we disconnect how we view ourselves from God's view of us, we neglect the deeper growth God desires. But when we align how we view ourselves with God's truth, we begin to see ourselves as tools to glorify him. We set boundaries and limits to refocus on rest—not because we are entitled to rest but because he calls us to it. These boundaries we set aren't meant to isolate us but to steward the time and energy we have for his purposes.

So if I were to rephrase Allie Beth's quote in the context of hospitality, it might sound something like this: "We're not enough—period. And that's okay, because God is. The answer to [our overwhelmed schedule, lonely life, and connection craving] isn't self-love, but God's love. In Jesus, we're offered a way out of our toxic culture of self-love and into a joyful life of relying on him for wisdom, satisfaction, and purpose [through the community that hospitality can provide]."[2]

Wow! There is so much freedom in that truth. As I wrote those words, I was reminded that God isn't looking for my perfection—he's looking for my participation. The beauty of hospitality isn't in the flawless table settings or the perfectly cooked meals; it's in showing up. It's not just about participating in the act of hospitality; it's also about participating in a relationship with God. The goal is to create boundaries so we can set aside time to seek intimacy with him. That doesn't happen in the chaos of life but in the quiet stillness of solitude with him.

So when we feel overwhelmed by our schedules or isolated in our longing for connection, the answer isn't found in striving harder or retreating into self-care. It's found in God's love—love that frees us to rely on him and equips us to share his goodness with others through the beautiful practice of hospitality.

How Do We Set Boundaries?

Establishing boundaries isn't about limiting generosity; establishing boundaries is about ensuring we have the capacity to offer hospitality freely and joyfully. By grounding ourselves in God's presence and prioritizing what sustains us, we can extend his love to others from a place of abundance instead of exhaustion. This foundation is essential as we step into the practice of opening our homes and hearts to others.

Without clear steps, it's easy to overcommit or lose sight of why we're inviting others into our lives in the first place. Setting boundaries doesn't mean shutting people out; it means building a framework that helps us steward our time, energy, and resources well. Here are three steps to help you establish boundaries that protect your heart, honor your season of life, and allow you to serve others from a place of abundance.

1. **Prioritize time with God.** To create healthy boundaries in your life, it's essential to carve out intentional moments with God. Whether it's through heartfelt prayer, diving into Scripture, or simply enjoying a quiet moment of reflection, these interactions can fill your heart and clarify your priorities. When you're spiritually grounded, you're better equipped to discern when to say yes and when to let go, ensuring

that your hospitality flows from his strength rather than your own.
2. **Define your capacity.** Remember, hospitality evolves through different seasons of life, so it's crucial to take stock of your current energy levels, resources, and schedule. Ask yourself, *How often can I host without feeling overwhelmed?* and *What kinds of gatherings align with my available time and budget?* By setting these parameters, you'll find it easier to say yes joyfully and no gracefully when the situation calls for it.
3. **Communicate clearly and kindly.** Establishing healthy boundaries often begins with open communication. It's helpful to share your limits with friends and family ahead of time to prevent any feelings of overwhelm. For instance, if you prefer hosting casual get-togethers over more elaborate events, don't hesitate to communicate that. Being up-front about your boundaries not only protects your peace but also nurtures mutual respect and understanding.

When Kyle and I were newly married, life felt complicated in ways I hadn't expected. We were learning how to navigate marriage, finances, and careers, all while juggling the nuanced expectations and pressures placed on newlyweds. I had dreamed of what hospitality would look like with other couples, sitting around the fire on the back porch with every seat at my table filled. And here I was, full table, lots of chatter, and a front door that was open to all, but I felt completely overwhelmed. I had fallen into the trap that the bigger the party, the more perfect the gathering—and the fuller my heart would be. But that wasn't the case. Hospitality didn't feel like a blessing anymore. Community was feeling more and more like a burden, and I wanted to just isolate myself.

One particularly hard week, I turned to God in desperation, and I asked him for clarity and strength. In the stillness, he reminded me that the connection I craved wasn't going to be satisfied through isolation or indulgence but through community with God and his people. He whispered to my heart that hospitality isn't just about serving others in large and grandiose dinner parties; it's about allowing his Spirit to move through simple and genuine connection with others. When we invite people in, he shows up, too, ushering in encouragement, edification, and joy that's not only for our guests but for us as well.

That realization shifted something in me; I'll never forget the first time I acted on the prompting from the Holy Spirit. It was a Thursday evening, and I was exhausted. I didn't have a meal planned or a sparkling clean house, but at 5:15 p.m. I sent a text to a couple of friends: "Bring your dinner over and let's eat together for an hour. Kyle will be home around 7." To my surprise, their responses were immediate: "On our way!" (Side note: Find people who say yes to your spontaneous asks and hold them close.)

We sat together at my kitchen table, ate mismatched meals, talked about life, and laughed until our stomachs hurt. It wasn't fancy, but it was exactly what my soul needed. I felt God's presence so clearly in that hour—his peace, his joy, and his reminder that we're not meant to do life alone. Hospitality wasn't just a gift I extended to my friends; it was his way of encouraging me through my tough season.

The Transformation

By prioritizing time with God, I learned to lean on his strength during seasons of weariness. Defining my capacity helped me let go of the pressure for a perfect meal or spotless home, embracing instead the beauty of spontaneity and authenticity. Finally, communicating my limits clearly—like letting my friends know to bring their own dinner—made the gathering not only manageable but joyful. These boundaries didn't restrict my ability to practice hospitality; they made it sustainable and fulfilling, even in the midst of life's complexities.

That night helped me realize that hospitality doesn't have to be over-the-top. I need to be willing to invite people into our home, our mess, and ultimately into the presence of the Holy Spirit. But before I could embrace this truth, I had to learn first the importance of boundaries and setting aside time with God. It was in those quiet moments sitting with God that I discovered how much I needed to be filled by his love and grace before I could pour them into others.

Creating space in my life to be with God—to listen, pray, and let him speak to my heart—helped me recognize that hospitality shouldn't be just another item on my to-do list. Instead, it needed to become a natural overflow of the time I spent with him. God showed me that when I say yes to him first, I'm able to create room in my life for what truly matters. Boundaries aren't meant to isolate or shut others out but to prioritize what strengthens us so that we can better serve God and love others well.

So when we feel overwhelmed by our schedules or isolated and in need of connection, the answer isn't found in striving harder or retreating into self-care. It's found in

God's love—love that frees us to rely on him and equips us to share his goodness with others through the beautiful practice of hospitality. When we draw close to him, he fills us with the wisdom and strength we need to invite others in—not from a place of exhaustion but from a place of rest.

Learning how to set boundaries in our lives is so important. God set up our world with boundaries, and Jesus was the perfect model for what a life of delicate balance looks like. I want to encourage you to set these physical and emotional boundaries in order to pursue a full life walking with God.

Setting Boundaries

In Christine Pohl's book *Making Room: Recovering Hospitality as a Christian Discipline,* she does such a good job at articulating what biblical hospitality looks like in Scripture and throughout history. When speaking about the challenges of showing hospitality, she wrote, "The practice of hospitality challenges the boundaries of a community while it simultaneously depends on that community's identity to make a space that nourishes life."[3] Practicing hospitality requires that we find a balance between community and solitude. We must honor our commitment to inviting and welcoming others and our responsibility to create space for our family and our relationship with God.

I've realized that setting boundaries around my hospitality is actually a good thing. It's not about shutting people out but creating a space where I can eagerly invite others for meaningful fellowship and to experience Christ's love in our home. I want my family to know that they are valued, my friends are welcome, and my door is always open. And at the end of the day, it's not just about having extra seats at my table. It's about making sure that as I open my home to others, my family still feels loved and nurtured. Balancing the two can definitely be challenging, especially as a new mom and only in my second year of marriage, but it's something I pray about regularly—that I'll grow in both my ability to serve others and my ability to care for those closest to me.

Not only did Jesus prioritize hospitality throughout his ministry by eating with tax collectors, feeding the five thousand, and dining with friends and family, but he also created boundaries. His actions remind us that boundaries are not just acceptable but essential for living a life focused on meaningful hospitality. When Lazarus, a close friend of Jesus and the brother of Mary and Martha, became seriously ill, his sisters urgently asked Jesus to come immediately. However, Jesus chose to wait two days before heading to Bethany. By the time he arrived, Lazarus had already been buried, leaving the sisters feeling frustrated and heartbroken (John 11:1–37). It would have been easy for Jesus to rush to their side, but he intentionally waited in order to demonstrate God's divine glory and his perfect and intentional timing. This shows us the importance of honoring our emotional boundaries. It's okay to say no or not yet when we need to focus on what God has called us to do.

Hospitality isn't about saying yes to every ask or situation. Instead, it's about creating a generous life that is sustainable and grounded in God's priorities. Just as Jesus set emotional and physical boundaries to bring the ultimate glory to God and protect what is sacred, we can also practice hospitality with healthy limits.

Emotional Boundaries

Jesus was willing to hang around with anyone. But no matter what the situation, no matter who he was with, he was always grounded in his identity as God's Son. Understanding what you believe in and what your identity is grounded in is key to healthy hospitality. No matter what our guests look like, how they vote, or where they come from, our hospitality should be inviting and welcoming. But here's the catch: Once you extend the invitation, you also take on the responsibility to establish emotional boundaries. It's important to remember that while we open our homes and our hearts, we do so in a way that reflects the love and respect Jesus shows us. You're not just welcoming guests into your home; you're welcoming them into a space that loves Jesus. And with that comes the responsibility to live by his example. This means that we don't gossip, we don't complain, we don't argue. The invitation is marked by truth and by having conversations bathed in Philippians 4:8: "Fix your thoughts on what is true, and honorable, and right, and pure, and lovely, and admirable. Think about things that are excellent and worthy of praise" (NLT).

I was a part of a community group a few years back that would recite this verse at the end of the opening prayer. We would all show up with our dinner and eat as we arrived, and then once everyone got there, we would pray over our time together. One person would pray intentionally for the

The Transformation

prayer requests and whatever we were studying, and after she said, "Amen," we'd all recite Philippians 4:8. Now that might sound weird. If you didn't grow up in a church that recited liturgy regularly, it might even be uncomfortable the first few times.

Reciting truth in Scripture during our time together helped set the tone of the evening. It provided boundaries for our conversations and guided our thoughts and emotions. What I appreciated most about these boundaries was that they made it clear to everyone present how and what we would talk about, especially those who were accustomed to gossiping or complaining. This healthy boundary allowed us to build a stronger community. While God welcomes everyone into his house, he also expects certain behaviors. As Christians we are guided by Scripture, not by the influence of others.

Ultimately, strong emotional boundaries make for a better welcome. That's certainly true in friendship and within our habit of hospitality. So before you even begin extending the invitation, ensure that you understand your emotional boundaries and can clearly communicate them.

Physical Boundaries

When I moved to northwest Arkansas in my late twenties, I was desperately looking for a community. I had tried several churches but couldn't find people who were similar to me: outgoing people who were my age or in the same stage of life, who loved Jesus, and who wanted to engage in activities. I knew my tribe was out there somewhere; I just needed to find them. As a Christian, it can sometimes feel like we're an

Serving Others Without Burning Out

enigma, but I was convinced that there were others like me around. It was just a matter of connecting with them.

After some searching, I found a group of women I enjoyed being around. They seemed fun and exciting, and the best part was that they loved the Lord. These women had been in a community group for a few years when I joined, so I knew it might be challenging to find exactly where I fit. I began inviting these new friends over, creating space for conversation, being an intentional listener, and trying hard to engage with them on a deeper level.

At first it was wonderful. I enjoyed getting to know this new group of women and loved having people I could pursue. However, after a few weeks I felt something aching in my heart and it was getting harder and harder to put in the effort. I was experiencing burnout. After months of extending hospitality to others, I realized I'd been focused on the needs of others and hadn't properly assessed my own needs.

Pohl reminisced on a time when her church was met with a similar situation: "Under the pressure of needs all around us, we were not careful to nourish our own lives, or to put [boundaries] in place that made sure [we] had adequate rest and renewal."[4]

Pohl's church, much like the environment I found myself in, did not create physical boundaries. These boundaries help create structure and define the balance between fellowship and solitude. Just as a parent might create boundaries for their children to determine freedom and structure, so we must institute them in our own habits and practices.

When we are walking lockstep with the Holy Spirit, who he is flows out of our hearts and minds (and mouths).

The Transformation

This divine connection cultivates an attitude of love and generosity that makes the practice of hospitality feel more effortless. As we reflect God's communal nature and embrace this calling to host, it's important to remember that we are not expected to be 100 percent hospitable at all times. Just as Jesus took moments to retreat and rest, we, too, need times of refreshment to recharge our spirits and maintain our well-being.

As you prepare to invite others into your space, take a moment to pause and reflect on the foundations of hospitality you have in place. The following assessment asks you to consider how your physical and emotional boundaries have prepared you for welcoming people into your home in a God-honoring way. Reflect on whether your boundaries contribute to creating a safe and comfortable atmosphere for your guests and think about what boundaries you may need to establish or strengthen to create a space that invites connection, fellowship, and joy.

EMOTIONAL BOUNDARIES

Do you feel genuinely called to extend this invitation at this time?
Reflect on whether this is the right time to extend hospitality. Pray for guidance and peace.

Serving Others Without Burning Out

Do you feel peace about inviting this person/group and not obligation?
Take a moment to consider your motives and check if there's an unhealthy sense of pressure. Pray and consider whether to proceed.

Are you clear on your own limitations (time, energy, capacity) and willing to communicate these kindly if needed?
Prayerfully consider what boundaries are needed. Remember that setting limits allows you to serve joyfully and be the hands and feet of Christ. You want your guests to see and experience Jesus, and they won't if your boundaries aren't clearly defined.

Do you know what you do and don't want to discuss?
Set boundaries on what topics are off-limits before guests arrive. Even if you don't communicate it to your guests ahead of time, be prepared to initiate a conversational diversion if topics arise that shouldn't be discussed.

Are you prepared for potential conflict or disagreements?
Think through how you might address sensitive issues or differing opinions if they arise, and ask God to give you the words, the tone, the attitude, and the empathy to respond in love.

The Transformation

PHYSICAL BOUNDARIES

Have you set a specific start and end time for the gathering?
Reflect on why setting a time frame is important. It helps manage expectations and allows for rest.

Do you know how many guests you can comfortably invite and host?
Consider your limits. Hosting too many can lead to overwhelm and fatigue.

Do you know how you need to prepare for this gathering?
Think about how a potluck or BYOFood night can lighten your load and give you time to engage with your guests. Consider also how complex meals can lead to stress.

Are you willing to delegate to create a physical boundary in your capacity?
Consider how sharing responsibilities can reduce stress and help you enjoy the get-together more.

Can you let go of perfectionism and the pressures that come with it?
Reflect on how striving for perfection can create stress. Embracing imperfection allows for a more genuine and enjoyable gathering experience.

Boundaries not only help define your personal space but also set clear expectations for your gatherings, ensuring that everyone understands where to go, what to expect, and how to engage. By creating a structured environment, you foster an atmosphere of respect and understanding, allowing your guests to feel welcomed while also protecting your own well-being.

Maintaining these boundaries is particularly important because they provide a necessary space for rest and refreshment for both you and your guests. When you prioritize your own needs alongside those of others, you establish a sustainable practice of hospitality that transforms your home into a place of joy and community, allowing you to embody the heart of Christ in your gatherings. Ultimately, respecting these emotional and physical boundaries enhances your ability to host, turning each gathering into a meaningful expression of love, service, and spiritual nourishment for everyone involved.

Hospitality Burnout

Our hospitality is ultimately constrained by our physical capacity. Drawing that physical boundary will always be a challenge because we are a people who are drawn to connection with others. God created us that way. I didn't realize I hadn't created that boundary until I looked up, and it was too late. I was burned out. In the process of creating a life marked by hospitality, we will always be toeing that fine line and trying to find the balance between community with others and our finite limitations.

The Transformation

In a culture that often places unrealistic expectations on us to be endlessly available and accommodating, it's important to remember that we don't have unlimited resources and God doesn't require that from us. Jesus serves as the perfect example of balance in hospitality, demonstrating a continual cycle of community and solitude. On one hand, he invited everyone to come to him: "Come to me, *all* you who are weary and burdened" (Matt. 11:28, emphasis mine). On the other hand, he made deliberate space in his life for solitude and rest, retreating to recharge and seek the Father. Jesus was not afraid to remove himself from the hordes of people to find solitude with God (Matt. 14:23) or kick the crowds out of the temple when they were disrespecting his Father's house (Matt. 21:12–13). He demonstrated the significant purpose of hospitality and the importance of creating boundaries to protect your relationship with God.

In our desire to emulate Christ's example, it's crucial to recognize the signs of hospitality burnout before they become overwhelming. When we continuously pour ourselves into hosting without allowing for personal time and rest, we risk depleting our emotional and spiritual reserves. This can lead to feelings of exhaustion and resentment rather than joy and fulfillment in our hospitality efforts. To help you discern if you might be experiencing hospitality burnout, consider the following eight warning signs:

1. **Overwhelming fatigue.** You feel physically and emotionally drained after hosting, even if the event was enjoyable in the moment.

Serving Others Without Burning Out

2. **Irritability.** Small inconveniences or challenges in hosting start to irritate you more than they should, affecting your mood and interactions.
3. **Dread of upcoming events.** Instead of looking forward to inviting people over, you feel anxious or dread the thought of people coming over, which in turn makes you irritable and quick-tempered.
4. **Neglecting personal needs.** You prioritize your guests' needs over your own well-being, often skipping meals, neglecting rest, or putting aside personal commitments.
5. **Lack of joy.** The joy you once felt in inviting others over has diminished, leaving you feeling indifferent or burdened by the responsibilities of hosting.
6. **Withdrawal from relationships.** You begin to isolate yourself from friends and family, opting out of social invitations that you would normally take part in due to feeling overwhelmed by your hosting obligations.
7. **Resentment.** You feel a growing sense of resentment toward hosting or toward guests, which can lead to negative thoughts about your hospitality efforts.
8. **Difficulty saying no.** You struggle to decline invitations or requests for hosting, even when you know you need a break, leading to feelings of being stretched too thin.

Jesus modeled the importance of solitude amid his communal ministry, and we must honor our own limitations. By intentionally carving out time for rest and reflection, we can create a healthier rhythm of hospitality that not only

The Transformation

nourishes our souls but also allows us to joyfully serve and connect with others. Remember, practicing hospitality should not come at the expense of your peace and well-being; it should be an expression of love that flows from a place of health and vitality.

Steps for Success

Now that we've discussed the importance of emotional and physical boundaries in hospitality, it's time to put those ideas into action. As you get ready to invite people into your space, thinking about who you want to invite and what boundaries you'd like to set can help you create a more enjoyable experience for everyone involved. The following steps serve as a handy guide, helping you think through your limits so you can offer genuine warmth while still taking care of yourself. By considering details like how long guests will stay, topics to avoid, and things you might do together, you'll lay the groundwork for meaningful connections without feeling overwhelmed. Setting these clear guardrails not only makes hosting more manageable but also creates an atmosphere where both you and your guests can relax and enjoy each other's company. So let's dive in together and make your hospitality experience a joyful one!

Step 1: Who are two or three people you can extend hospitality to on a frequent basis?

When I started my practice of hospitality and exercising those spiritual muscles, I was a young single looking for a community. When I got engaged there was a moment where I grieved my singleness, because I loved the habit of hospitality I had developed. I could be spontaneous and have people over whenever. I didn't have someone else's schedule to consider. I had all the flexibility. I am now in a very different place in my life—married with a child—and there is something so sweet about having a family and developing a new habit of hospitality with them.

Whatever stage of life you find yourself in, whether single or married, there will be challenges you will have to figure out. But I would highly encourage you to get out of the rut of inviting only people in the same stage of life as you into your space. Invite those older and more mature to speak wisdom into your life or find those singles in your community you can pour into.

As you extend invitations, remember to establish both physical and emotional boundaries to protect your well-being and create a welcoming atmosphere. These boundaries can help define the dynamics of your get-togethers, ensuring that everyone feels respected and comfortable.

Step 2: What does the cadence of hospitality in your life look like?

This step is about finding a balance between offering hospitality and maintaining your well-being, making sure you can invite others in without overextending yourself. If hospitality isn't something you practice regularly, it can feel a bit daunting at the beginning. Don't feel like you need to go from zero to sixty in two weeks. We can go from zero to two in two weeks, or we can go from zero to five.

The Transformation

What does your capacity look like? Have you identified your physical boundaries? Do you have limitations regarding time or location? By understanding these boundaries, you create a sustainable approach to hospitality that doesn't overwhelm you.

Then, once you've built up some of the muscle memory required for hospitality, start practicing it twice a month. When you've built up the muscles a little bit more, start practicing it once a week. Hospitality, while not my spiritual gift, was easy for me to put into practice. The muscle memory was there because I had walked alongside my mom, aunts, and grandmothers as they extended hospitality to others. After getting married, my ability to be hospitable was influenced not only by my schedule and flexibility but also by my spouse's preferences regarding guests in our home. I had to recognize and respect our differing desires and limits and learn how to practice hospitality while considering Kyle's boundaries. This collaboration on our physical boundaries not only strengthened our relationship but also enriched our hospitality experiences, allowing us to welcome others into our home with joy and intention. The cadence of your hospitality should be something that fits into everyone's rhythm and routine.

Step 3: What's the purpose and goal?

When you have a clear intention behind your invitation—whether it's to deepen a friendship, offer support during a difficult time, or create space for spiritual growth—that sets the stage for God to move in big ways. This clarity not only helps guide the conversation and activities while you are together but also enables you to prepare your heart and mind to be fully present. By being intentional about the purpose of your hospitality, you invite others to engage with that same intention, creating an environment ripe for authentic connection and shared experiences.

It's also beneficial to clearly define emotional boundaries in the context of your hospitality goals. Establishing these boundaries allows you to communicate openly about what is and isn't acceptable during your time together, ensuring that everyone feels safe and respected. Emotional guardrails help both you and your guests understand the purpose of the get-together and enhances the overall experience, paving the way for genuine connections rooted in love, respect, and mutual understanding.

• • • • •

Now, I have one piece of advice for the singles reading this book—this goes for my divorced and widowed friends too: Invite yourself over to others' homes. It's hard for married couples with children to get everyone together and come to your space, but it's usually easier for you to go over to their homes. I have a friend who recently experienced a divorce later in life, and one thing she has started doing is inviting herself over to my house to love on me while I am taking care of John Maverick. It is such a blessing. Not only is she pouring her wisdom into me while she is here but she is so encouraging, and she also runs around my house like a little fairy and picks up odds and ends. So I say this to encourage

The Transformation

you: People generally love it when others extend hospitality in their own space.

I'm guessing if you picked up this book, this is a hard step for you. It might even be uncomfortable. I am praying for you now that God has placed a few people in your life that you can begin practicing hospitality on. Just like Peter took a few steps in faith out on the waves (Matt. 14:29), these are your steps outside your comfort zone. By putting ourselves outside our comfort zone, we position ourselves to live out the gospel faithfully within the community where God has placed us.

That's why we set boundaries—so we can hear God better and, therefore, share his love more. Boundaries protect us from burnout, ensuring that our hospitality flows from a heart that's full, not depleted. They create the margin we need to rest in God's presence and refocus on what truly matters: a life marked by loving him and inviting others in. When we prioritize time with God and honor the limits he's given us, we're better equipped to extend his love in meaningful ways. Setting boundaries isn't about holding back; it's about creating the space for a life of intentionality, joy, and genuine connection, a life that glorifies him through the rhythm of hospitality.

Chapter 11

• • • • •

The Legacy of Your Table

As I think back on where my legacy of hospitality started, I think about twenty feet of card tables covered with red gingham plastic tablecloths lined up in the rec room at my grandmother's house. It was a room added on to the house, and it boasted vinyl flooring, doors that opened to a large patio, and a pool table that I don't remember once being used for pool (instead, it served as the buffet for our food—always with a large piece of plywood and a tablecloth covering the top). This large room was the center of my grandmother's home. She had parties, luncheons, cookouts—you name it—in this downstairs rec room.

It's where we had Sunday lunch every week. It's where I celebrated birthdays and learned the importance of the table. Not just my grandmother's table that I grew up sitting

The Transformation

around with my family, which I still remember fondly, but *the* table. The table is a place where we can all come no matter our differences and be met with love and attention. The concept of coming to the table together signifies a shared experience, a breaking down of barriers, and a coming together as one. This inclusive nature of the table is evident in the New Testament, where Jesus often dined with sinners and outcasts, demonstrating his love and acceptance for all. The table, therefore, becomes a tangible representation of God's grace and his desire for all people to come together. The table extends a welcome no matter what you are going through, and it encourages you with wisdom and truth. The table I sat around for most of my life was one of inclusion and where I saw aunts and uncles, cousins, and grandparents leave a legacy of hospitality.

This was a normal occurrence. Christine Pohl wrote it this way: "In a hospitable household, conversation and meals are closely linked, and people are nourished through both."[1] I saw my family, friends, acquaintances, and people I didn't know walk through those doors, my grandparents intent on making each person feel valued, seen, and known. That was how I learned to show love. Our homes are the most personal settings into which we can invite people. And it was modeled for me that welcoming people into our homes and our lives should be a second-nature extension of our faith.

For my family, hospitality wasn't just a one-time thing; it was a way of life. My grandparents' example influenced their children, who grew up in an environment where intentional generosity was valued. My mom and her siblings witnessed firsthand the joy and fulfillment that come from opening your home to others. This instilled a desire to continue the tradition, creating a legacy that would be passed down to their children (me!) and grandchildren. The hospitality my mom and aunts and uncles demonstrated fostered a sense of biblical community and promoted a deeper, more intimate relationship with Jesus, creating a legacy that is being passed down through generations.

I believe we can change generations too. People will walk into your living room faster than they will walk into a church, and hospitality is the tool we can use to invite others to experience Christ. I believe that by practicing hospitality and refining the art of the invite, we are walking a God-ordained path to living out the gospel through our everyday habits and creating spaces to change people's lives forever.

Transformative Hospitality

Leaving a legacy of hospitality is about more than just a single act of kindness. It is about creating a culture of hospitality within our communities and families. It is about being the example of intentional hospitality and the welcoming of others and making them feel at home. When we do this, we are not only leaving a legacy for ourselves but also for future generations.

We read examples of generational hospitality in the New Testament as we reflect on early church history. The early church left us a rich "hospitality as discipleship" legacy. In other words, the church didn't rely on intense sermons

The Transformation

and pamphlet passing to invite others to Christ. They used hospitality; they welcomed people into their homes to experience Jesus firsthand. It was a ministry of care, compassion, and meeting the needs of those who accepted the invitation. And the results were life-changing.

When Jesus returned after his resurrection, he told his disciples, "Go and make disciples of all the nations" (Matt. 28:19 NLT). This is the Great Commission, which I reframed in chapter 9 as the Great Invite. The early church soon exploded in growth, and by the middle of the first century there were churches popping up everywhere. If the early church exploded in growth after obeying the Great Commission, how much could our communities explode in Christian love if we were to obey the Great Invite and welcome people to experience Jesus at our table?

The key to leaving a legacy of hospitality that transforms generations is to welcome all to the table. We are called to welcome everyone to experience Jesus even deeper. Even if it doesn't occur immediately, we open the door for their intimacy with Christ to flourish. You can't control what your guests receive out of the invitation, but you can control your obedience to the command.

When we take seriously the possibility that people can belong before they believe, we are given the freedom to reimagine what it means to be the church today. Don't get me wrong. Knowing and believing are imperative. Let's look at the example Jesus left us. Throughout the New Testament we see him including the outsiders, especially those who didn't believe in him: the Samaritan woman, the tax collectors, the prostitutes, the lepers, and even the

The Legacy of Your Table

demon possessed. He invited them in, ate with them, and spoke to them when everyone else looked the other way. Inviting people to sit at your table is not about accepting the sin people live in; it's about accepting the people despite the sin.

Our culture today tells us the false message that we should "live your own truth" and "you are perfect just the way you are." The gospel invites everyone to come as they are, but it doesn't stop there. The message of the gospel we share at our tables is different. The gospel tells us that God loves us, but also that, on our own, we'll never be good enough. It's only through Jesus that we are made worthy, healed, and transformed. In every single instance of people accepting the invite Jesus extended in Scripture, they walked away changed. That is the type of legacy and impact your invite can have through transformative hospitality. More often than not people come to Jesus not because they are forced to or because they are given a hellfire-and-brimstone ultimatum but because they received genuine love from a Christian.

Without inviting God to the table, without pursuing his purpose for our welcome, our hospitality falls on deaf ears. It only has the divine power to change lives when we invite the sovereign God to join us at the table.

Those who live out transformative hospitality see their tables as God's gift to use to welcome all in—not just to their home but to the kingdom of God. They open doors, they seek out the outsider, and they allow the Holy Spirit to cover outsiders in his love. We are just the hands and feet of God; we have a job to do. And this gives us the opportunity

The Transformation

to leave a legacy that doesn't just change someone's life on earth but for eternity. So we *must* seek to invite all to the table to experience that life-changing redemption.

David and Amy White are a couple from my town who shared a video on Instagram about a tradition they started called Waffles at 10. They invited their son's friends over on Friday nights following football games to create an environment that was safe for high schoolers—because nothing good happens after dark, am I right? It started small with a few friends a couple of nights a year. Soon Waffles at 10 exploded to include girlfriends, parents, and friends of friends.[2]

The Whites' unwavering commitment to opening their home fostered a deep sense of inclusivity and belonging, creating a warm and inviting space where kids from all walks of life were embraced. Waffles at 10 transcended the simple act of enjoying breakfast at bedtime, and it became a meaningful platform for sharing God's love and affectionately nurturing friendships in the home on Friday nights.

This example of transformative hospitality didn't stop within the walls of Amy and David's home; #wafflesat10 became a powerful catalyst that inspired and encouraged others to extend the same warm welcome within their homes. Soon more environments formed where the love of God permeated and worked its transformative wonders.

David and Amy's consistency in obedience of hospitality set an extraordinary example. Feeding a bunch of growing teenagers can get expensive, but the Whites viewed this time not merely as a meal but also as a powerful avenue to connect people with the love of Christ. Suddenly the cost seemed trivial and insignificant. How much would you spend to know someone's life would forever change and they would spend eternity in heaven?

Think about it: What did God use to draw people to him? Was it a huge conference or event? A celebrity or a well-spoken evangelist? No, God used an invitation from a humble couple living out the gospel authentically to eat waffles after a high school football game.

Hospitality is not some stuffy, outdated practice. It is the gospel in action. If hospitality is so important to God, then it must be practiced as the "primary way we tell the astounding story that God hasn't given up on us. Any time we practice hospitality we follow in the steps of our lavishly hospitable God."[3] That is what David and Amy did. They practiced hospitality in the simplest way, inviting people into their home to eat. It was casual and unassuming. From the outside it might have even looked easy. But they took the small step of obedience, welcoming people in to eat and experience the love of God. It's how we saw Jesus do ministry, and it shouldn't come as a surprise that when we model that same behavior, inviting all who will come in, we see lives changed. That is the transformative hospitality of Christ leaving a lasting legacy.

So how do we do that? How do we leave a legacy of hospitality?

How to Leave a Legacy

Leaving this type of legacy takes time and sacrifice, but it can be achieved by reaching out to the people God has

The Transformation

put in your sphere of influence and finding opportunities to care for them. You can leave a legacy of hospitality by simply doing the little things.

A legacy of hospitality requires a mindset of stewardship with our resources—we are intentional about our time, our money, our relationships, and how we use them all to impact others. Scripture shows that this mindset has always been God's plan for passing on his truth from generation to generation:

- "So even to old age and gray hairs, O God, do not forsake me, until I proclaim your might to another generation, your power to all those to come" (Ps. 71:18 ESV).
- "We will tell the next generation the praiseworthy deeds of the LORD, his power, and the wonders he has done" (Ps. 78:4).
- "Let this be written for a future generation, that a people not yet created may praise the LORD" (Ps. 102:18).
- "One generation commends your works to another; they tell of your mighty acts" (Ps. 145:4).

As we cultivate a spirit of hospitality, it's essential to involve the younger generations in our journey. By including our children and grandchildren in our hospitality practices, we not only pass down the values of kindness and service but also empower them to continue this legacy in their own lives. Here are six creative ways to engage your family in the art of hospitality, ensuring that the

The Legacy of Your Table

heart of welcoming others becomes an integral part of their lives as well.

1. **Neighborly acts of kindness kits.** Help your children create kindness kits filled with simple items like homemade baked goods, handwritten notes of encouragement, or small gifts like a coffee cup from the dollar section at Target and a tea bag. Then plan a day where you and your kids deliver these kits to neighbors, sharing the love of Christ.
2. **Community potluck planning.** Organizing a fun community potluck with your kids and grandkids is a great way to get everyone involved. You can have the kids help plan everything from designing the invitations to setting up the tables. As you prepare, encourage them to think about how to make guests feel welcomed and valued. This hands-on experience is all about sharing meals and enjoying fellowship, and it'll really drive home the joy of hospitality.

    Some communities even have potluck food trucks that make this process super easy. You might consider rallying a group of kids to volunteer at one of these food trucks or even at a local shelter. This way, they'll learn that hospitality isn't just about inviting family and friends over; it's also about reaching out to those in the wider community. It's a wonderful opportunity for them to see the impact of kindness beyond their own circle.
3. **Scripture scavenger hunt.** Create a scavenger hunt using Scripture verses about hospitality, love, and

The Transformation

service. Each clue can lead to a neighbor's house, where they can deliver a small gift or a note with a relevant verse attached. This fun and interactive activity reinforces biblical teaching while allowing children to practice hospitality in a tangible way.

When I lived in Columbia, South Carolina, I organized several of these Scripture scavenger hunts in my apartment complex with some neighbors I'd met. I created clues based on verses about hospitality, love, and service, each leading to a different door. One clue with Luke 12:27, "Consider the lilies, how they grow" (ESV), led to a door with a floral wreath. At the door we left a sticky note with Psalm 34:8, "Taste and see that the LORD is good," and a blessing bag of chocolate chip cookies.

On these Scripture scavenger hunts, we'd knock, drop off six to eight blessing bags, share our message of love, and call it a night. It was such a joy to bless others with random acts of kindness while sharing God's goodness.

4. **Hospitality skills workshops.** Organize fun days at home with your children where they can learn practical hospitality skills such as setting the table, greeting guests, and even basic cooking. These workshops build confidence and instill a sense of responsibility and ownership in welcoming others.

5. **Story-sharing nights.** It's so important to impart truth to our kids and grandchildren and to help them verbalize it and teach it to each other. Set aside time for family story-sharing nights where you read and

discuss Bible stories that emphasize hospitality, like the Good Samaritan or Jesus feeding the five thousand. Afterward, brainstorm ways your family can embody these stories in real life by inviting neighbors over for a meal, offering help, or simply spending time together. Encourage your children to think creatively about how they can extend hospitality in their own unique ways.

6. **Family welcome committee.** Create a welcome committee with your children and grandchildren. Assign roles—such as greeter, activity coordinator, or helper—to make everyone feel involved. The kids can help set up the space, welcome guests at the door, and introduce them to others, ensuring that no one feels left out. By role-playing and teaching children how to greet, include, coordinate, and participate, you are training your children how to be involved and intentional with people they invite over or meet when they are out at someone else's home.

Training up our children and grandchildren to have a spirit of biblical hospitality is so important. As they witness and engage in the joy of welcoming guests, they learn to reflect God's love and grace in their own lives. This practice not only cultivates a legacy of hospitality that honors our calling as believers but also creates opportunities for meaningful relationships, both within the family and with those we invite into our home, and thus we are impacting generations to come in both our family and others' families.

The Transformation

Ultimately, sharing the table as we embody the heart of Christ in our hospitality becomes a powerful act of service that teaches our children the importance of community and the transformative impact of gathering together in love and faith. Because at the end of the day, our table isn't about us. It's not about the plates we've set, it's not about the hot-and-ready food, and it isn't even about the worship music we have serenading us on our speakers. It's about Jesus. The sooner we can humble ourselves and admit that it's not by our strength but Christ's that people can sit at our table and receive life-giving change, the faster we will find ourselves bathing in his blessing.

That's why I loved the idea of naming this book *Let the Biscuits Burn*. It was important to me that this not be a book presenting itself as an expert's guide to hospitality but rather a book that declares loudly that it's okay not to have it all together. It's okay not to be enough, because we serve a God who, despite the chaos and imperfections of our lives, chooses to show up and show out. He asks for our hearts, not perfect biscuits. James 4:10 says, "Humble yourselves before the Lord, and he will lift you up."

When we are humble, we are reminded that we are all the same—sinful and finite, lacking everything, and fully reliant on God. Humility leads to joy, because it frees us up to throw off the distraction of perfection and connect with others.

When we humble ourselves before God, recognize our limitations, and allow him to teach and guide us, we experience a joy we never knew was possible. It's this joy that shines through our love for community and the people we welcome to our table. Every time we welcome others with joyful hospitality through prayer and humility, we are saying that even though this is a simple act that feels inadequate, it is what God will use to change the world. Because all things work together for good for those who love God and are called according to his purpose (Rom. 8:28). As we strive to cultivate a habit of hospitality, let me point you toward something Jesus said: "Anyone who welcomes you welcomes me, and anyone who welcomes me welcomes the one who sent me" (Matt. 10:40).

Grounding ourselves in the spiritual discipline of hospitality allows us to focus inward on our heart and develop an intimacy with Christ that draws others in to experience him at our table. By investing ourselves in this type of biblical hospitality, we can create a space for true fellowship and connection that transforms lives and leaves a legacy.

So let us be like Mary, sitting at the feet of Jesus, listening to his words, and being fully present in the moment. Let us create a space where everyone feels seen and valued—where the outsider becomes an insider and those who gather around your table experience the love of God in a way that lingers long after the meal is over.

Because here's the truth in hospitality: Every meal shared, every conversation sparked, and every invitation extended is leaving a legacy. You are showing your friends, your kids, your family, and anyone who enters your home what it looks like to welcome others as Christ has welcomed us. Just like Christ doesn't require us to be perfect to enter his home, he doesn't require our hospitality to be perfect either. It's not the biscuits people will remember; it's how

The Transformation

they felt in your presence and how they experienced God's love through you.

Let us focus on the people at our table, pouring our hearts into the relationships being formed, so much so that we don't even notice the biscuits burning in the oven.

Conclusion

• • • • • • •

Let's Do the Next Hard Thing

Let's talk about doing the next hard thing—to glorify God through excellence and faith. God is honored when we choose obedience, even in the tough moments. As James 1:2–3 says, "Consider it pure joy, my brothers and sisters, whenever you face trials of many kinds, because you know that the testing of your faith produces perseverance." Our calling as Christians isn't always easy, but it's the only calling worthy of the hard. In Matthew 11:28 Jesus invited us to "come to me, all you who are weary and burdened, and I will give you rest." But he doesn't leave us there. We're also called to take up our cross and follow him and to embrace

Conclusion

challenges that shape and refine us. Romans 5:3–4 tells us, "We also glory in our sufferings, because we know that suffering produces perseverance; perseverance, character; and character, hope." Just like King Saul resisted God's process in 1 Samuel, we can get in the way of God's plans if we avoid the uncomfortable transformation he has for us. But when we trust him, even in those difficult moments, it makes all the difference, and he gets the glory.

Has anyone ever told you that God designed us to do hard things? That he actually commanded us to do hard things? Philippians 4:13 says, "I can do all this through him who gives me strength." It's not something many people want to hear, though. In today's world we're all about convenience, always looking for ways to make life easier. First John 2:16 reminds us, "For everything in the world—the lust of the flesh, the lust of the eyes, and the pride of life—comes not from the Father but from the world," and these can distract us from the growth God wants to bring about in us.

Take something as simple as grocery shopping. Now we have apps that do the hard work for us. Someone shops for us, delivers the groceries to our car, and sometimes even to our front door. I've even heard people wish the delivery person would put the groceries away for them! And believe it or not, some services do offer this now.

We're a culture obsessed with making things easier, but God's call often leads us through hard things that refine us, shape our character, and grow our faith. Romans 8:28 says, "And we know that in all things God works for the good of those who love him, who have been called according to his purpose."

Conclusion

We avoid inconvenience at all costs. We don't like doing the next hard thing. But in Scripture, we can't avoid it. For example, when Jesus commanded us to love our enemies (Luke 6:27), why can't we just do it? Because it's hard. Forgiving is hard. Turning the other cheek is hard. Speaking the truth is hard. Not gossiping is hard. Sharing the gospel is hard. Meditating on his Word is hard. The list goes on.

But if we are striving to live a life that is glorifying to God by practicing the spiritual discipline of hospitality, shouldn't these things be easy? We have an entire playbook of yeses and noes, rights and wrongs, do this and not that, and we still can't seem to follow directions.

When we restrain ourselves, when we give in to the hard and give up, God isn't glorified. He isn't glorified when we say, "It's too hard" or "I'll try again later." He is glorified when we put forth the effort to proclaim the gospel and invite others in. That's where we leave our legacy. Pushing through the hard with extraordinary effort and bringing people to God's table to experience his love.

The kind of dedication described here has been proven throughout history to lead to the best life, but it's not easy. The people we read about, meet, and may even know who have devoted their lives to serving God and put all their effort into practicing hospitality didn't shy away from difficulty. Instead, they embraced it and, as a result, experienced a deep connection with Christ that comes only from being obedient in uncomfortable situations.

I guarantee that when you begin practicing hospitality, stop making excuses, and begin looking for ways to love and serve others, you will experience joy from the Holy

Conclusion

Spirit that our culture cannot manufacture. Avoiding hard hospitality will only result in a life devoid of the blessing God eagerly wants to give you. Following in Jesus' footsteps and practicing hospitality like he did is hard, but it's so good when you do it. He is the ultimate example of the legacy we can leave when we extend the welcome to the outsider, love the stranger, and get uncomfortable.

The church I attend has a saying: "Our fingerprints should be everywhere, and our name should be nowhere." I love that because it's not about the quality of your hospitality, the decorations in your home, or the taste of your food. Instead my church's saying communicates, "Let the biscuits burn and let God's love shine." Do the hard thing, invite someone in, and let God do the rest. This can be your best life—not the easiest or the most convenient—if you decide to pick up your cross and follow God.

Committing to God and taking up your cross every day isn't about convenience or being comfortable; it's about surrendering your plans, your desires, and your comfort zones, and trusting that his plan is far better. It's a big ask, but I promise the reward is worth it. An invitation to your table isn't just about sharing a meal; it's an opportunity to be a tool in God's hands, allowing him to use you to impact someone's life in ways you may never fully see. It can be hard to trust God when he pushes us outside of our comfort zone, but that hard means we're letting go of our limitations and allowing his infinite power to work in ways that are far beyond our understanding. And having the opportunity to be used by God to change someone's life forever—that hard—is good.

Liturgy for Your Heart

One thing that helps me when I'm trying to pray through something is to write out a Scripture-based liturgy. Liturgies help ground our desires, prayers, and petitions to the Lord in truth. We all need a constant recentering on Christ, and the practice of repeating Scripture and truth helps guide our minds back to experiencing him in our day-to-day lives.

I've written a liturgy here for us to center our minds around living an authentic life with other believers through the daily habit of hospitality. Earmark this page, take a picture of it with your phone, or write it out on a sticky note to pray over as you begin this journey of reimagining the habit of hospitality in your own life.

> The Lord will fulfill his purpose for me;
>   your steadfast love, O Lord,
> endures forever.

Liturgy for Your Heart

> Do not forsake the work of your hands.
>
> PSALM 138:8 ESV

I come before you with a heart filled with gratitude. Your love and grace are boundless, and I am humbled by your presence in my life. As Jesus welcomed all who came to him, may I, too, extend hospitality to those around me. Let my home be a place of warmth and welcome, where others feel loved and valued. Remove anything that hinders me from inviting people to experience your grace and kindness, and may my welcome be a testament to your goodness and love. As I go out into the world today, may people hear your voice in my words and see your love in my actions. Grant me the wisdom and courage to serve you faithfully.

> Teach me your ways, O LORD,
> that I may live according to your truth!
> Grant me purity of heart,
> so that I may honor you.
> With all my heart I will praise you, O Lord my God.
> I will give glory to your name forever,
> for your love for me is very great.
> You have rescued me from the depths of death.
>
> PSALM 86:11–13 NLT

Liturgy for Your Heart

Lord, we see the absurdity of our pursuit of perfection in light of your creation. We confess that we have not always been hospitable or welcomed others with open arms. We have been self-centered and focused on our own needs. Forgive us for our shortcomings. Help us to develop a hospitable heart that reflects your love for all people. Grant us the grace to invite others to your table and to share the good news of your love.

Keep on loving each other as brothers and sisters. Don't forget to show hospitality to strangers, for some who have done this have entertained angels without realizing it!
Hebrews 13:1–2 NLT

You are the epitome of hospitality, a God unlike any other. Your open arms and welcoming table invite all to come to you. You have made a home for us in your kingdom and provided everything we need. Help me to be disciplined in serving others and showing hospitality to all. Lord, I pray that by living a life marked by hospitality, I would reflect your goodness and draw others to you.

Contribute to the needs of the saints and seek to show hospitality.
Romans 12:13 ESV

I desire to reflect you. Open my heart to the needs of others, and empower me to offer hospitality without hesitation. May my home be a place of comfort and solace so that no matter what circumstances people find themselves in, my table would welcome them just like the example you gave by welcoming us to your table.

God is able to make all grace abound to you, so that having all sufficiency in all things at all times, you may abound in every good work.

2 CORINTHIANS 9:8 ESV

Lord, there is no one like you. Your love, generosity, and hospitality are beyond comparison. We are so grateful for your presence that works in us and through us to share your kingdom with the world.

Thank you for your Son, who opened the doors wide and broke down the barriers that kept people from experiencing your love.

May our homes become extensions of your kingdom, places where your love is felt and experienced. Help us to be known not for our perfect appearances but for our open hearts and welcoming spirits.

In Jesus' name, amen.

Table Tips

Sometimes when we don't think we can do something well, like inviting someone into our home, we overthink it. Hospitality isn't meant to be fussy or fancy. It's meant to be *friendly*. So the best piece of advice I can give you as you embark on this journey is to think like a guest.

Would you like an extra-long phone-charger cord in a room you're staying in? If you answered yes, why not provide one for your guest?

Would you enjoy caviar on top of a crudité platter with smoked Alaskan salmon? If the answer is no, pop in some Totino's Pizza Rolls and enjoy the conversation!

Don't overcomplicate the organic. Let conversation run freely, and allow God to move through the space and use your hospitality to impact lives for the kingdom.

But you came here for a how-to on hospitality. In the following pages you'll find some of my tried-and-true

Table Tips

recipes, things I always keep stocked in my pantry for those last-minute guests, helpful resources, and my top-ten hospitality tips and tricks to make your journey to second-nature hospitality a breeze.

Pantry Staple List

Keeping a few ready-to-use items on hand can make all the difference when you're short on time but want your guests to feel at home. Here's a list of my pantry and fridge staples, with some well-loved time-saving ideas to help you create easy and crowd-pleasing snacks or meals in a pinch.

1. PILLSBURY CRESCENT ROLLS

These buttery rolls are incredibly versatile. You can make everything from classic rolls to quick appetizers to even desserts.

Wrap around mini sausages for easy pigs in a blanket, add cheese and garlic for savory twists, or fill with chocolate chips for a fast dessert. Great for both kids and adults!

2. TOTINO'S PIZZA ROLLS

Pizza rolls are a perfect appetizer or snack for any gathering. Just pop them in the oven or air fryer for a quick, crowd-pleasing option.

Serve with marinara or ranch as a dip, or for a fun

Table Tips

twist, sprinkle some grated Parmesan and fresh basil on top before serving.

3. RITZ CRACKERS
A classic choice with endless possibilities. They're great for building snack boards, and you can even use them as a base for mini appetizers.

Top with cheese and sliced cherry tomatoes for a quick bite, spread with peanut butter and a drizzle of honey, or make mini cracker sandwiches with ham and cheese.

4. VELVEETA CHEESE
Velveeta melts smoothly, making it ideal for cheesy dips and quick comfort foods.

Make a savory app by mixing browned sausage with Velveeta, then spooning the mixture generously on top of rye bread and baking until bubbly and golden.

5. CAMPBELL'S CREAM OF MUSHROOM SOUP
A pantry classic for casseroles, dips, and one-pot dishes.

Combine with pasta, shredded chicken, and frozen veggies for a quick casserole; or make a creamy sauce for baked chicken. It's a great shortcut for adding richness to any dish.

6. STACY'S PITA CHIPS
These chips are perfect for building a snack board.

They're sturdy enough to serve with creamy dips and spreads. Pair with hummus, spinach artichoke dip, or bruschetta.

Table Tips

7. RO-TEL
A must-have for adding quick spice and flavor.

Stir into queso, mix into soups or chilis, or use as a topping for tacos and nachos. Ro-tel adds a kick and depth of flavor to almost any dish.

8. FROZEN MEATBALLS
Frozen meatballs make it easy to throw together a hearty appetizer or main dish in minutes, and the Italian style are so yummy.

Heat with marinara sauce and serve with toothpicks or toss them in BBQ sauce for a sweet and savory snack. You can also serve them on sliders with cheese and marinara for a quick twist on meatball subs.

9. FANCY MAC 'N' CHEESE
A quick, comforting option that you can dress up with a few add-ins. I like the White Cheddar Macaroni & Cheese from Good & Gather or Great Value's Artisan Crafted Italian Five Cheese.

Mix in cooked bacon or green onions for a flavorful twist or stir in some hot sauce and shredded cheese for extra creaminess. It's a hit with kids but can be elevated for adults too.

10. TORTILLA CHIPS
A must-have for instant snacking. Tortilla chips pair well with so many dips and toppings.

Serve with salsa, guacamole, or queso; or make

a quick tray of nachos by adding shredded cheese, black beans, and Ro-tel. Perfect for casual entertaining.

11. PEPPERIDGE FARM PUFF PASTRY

A little fancy but incredibly versatile and easy to work with if you keep some in the freezer.

Wrap around brie for baked brie, make quick pastries by filling with jam, or create savory tarts with cheese and veggies.

12. FROZEN FRENCH FRIES OR TATER TOTS

A crowd-pleasing side or snack option.

Bake or air fry and serve with ketchup, aioli, or cheese sauce. You can also turn them into loaded fries with cheese, sour cream, and green onions.

13. HUMMUS

A ready-to-go dip that's great for veggies, pita, or crackers. Sabra is the go-to hummus in my house.

Serve with pita chips, carrots, and celery; or use it as a spread in wraps and sandwiches. You can even top it with a drizzle of olive oil and paprika for a more elegant presentation.

14. PILLSBURY GRANDS! BISCUITS

These fluffy biscuits are ideal for breakfast, brunch, or a side with dinner.

Serve with jam or honey or bake them as a side for soup. You can also flatten them, add pizza sauce and toppings, and make mini-pizzas.

Table Tips

15. MINUTE RICE

A speedy way to make rice when you need a quick side or meal base.

Pair with stir-fried veggies and a splash of soy sauce or serve with beans and salsa for an easy Tex–Mex bowl. Minute Rice is perfect for building quick, filling meals.

• • • • •

These items bring variety to your pantry, making it easy to put together snacks, appetizers, or even main courses without much fuss. Whether you're serving kids, adults, or anyone in between, these staples make serving (and inviting) last-minute guests a breeze.

Handy Household Items

Building up your collection of entertaining essentials can take some time, but this list will help you get started. The key to selecting ceramic dinnerware is choosing basic white pieces. White has a timeless quality that pairs well with any style, lets the food take center stage, and seamlessly coordinates, giving your setup a polished, cohesive look.

- Large porcelain platters for turkeys, large entrees, or big quantities of appetizers.

Table Tips

- Medium trays and small trays for various appetizers and desserts.
- Big bowls and medium bowls for salads, chips, or crackers.
- 8-ounce minibowls or ramekins for dips, spreads, olives, or trail mix. We love keeping a stack of fun and different-patterned bowls next to our trail mix canister so we are always ready to serve.
- Charcuterie board, and make sure it has a lip on it. You'll thank me when you are trying to move it from place to place in your house.
- Cheese knives, serving utensils, and mini-tongs. I like to purchase these in bulk from Amazon because they can be super inexpensive. I have three tongs of different sizes, so no matter what food I'm serving, I've got it covered.
- Baskets. Add a colorful napkin inside to serve bread and crackers, or use them to hold plastic flatware on the table.

What to Do with the Table

Think of a table setting like layering a cozy, stylish outfit. Each layer—chargers, plates, flatware, and glassware—adds style, texture, and character. Here's a simple way to create a trendy or timeless look for any occasion, no matter your experience level.

Table Tips

1. **Start with a charger (or multiple).** Silver or gold chargers add a touch of elegance that pairs beautifully with almost any theme, while woven chargers have a more organic feel. Just remember to center each charger where the guest's plate will go, making sure it's just a few inches from the edge of the table.
2. **Layer your plates.** Invest in white and mix your shapes and sizes. Don't shy away from square or oval for contrast. My favorite place setting is a flat leafy square placemat, with a dark brown and round rattan charger, with a white plate and a square app plate on top. I love the textures and shapes. It gives the table so much personality.
3. **Finish the place setting with the flatware and glasses.** Place the flatware on each side of the plate, with forks to the left and knives and spoons to the right. For the glasses, I like to include the drinking glass and a coffee mug or teacup. Since I don't drink alcohol, the coffee cup helps add dimension and gives a progression for the evening, so my guests know that I will be offering a drink with dessert.
4. **For the centerpiece,** I often prefer using candles instead of fresh flowers or greenery, and I like to place them on a runner. There are plenty of examples and tutorials available on YouTube and Pinterest, so I encourage you to explore those resources. Remember, when it comes to

Table Tips

centerpieces, less is often more. You want to ensure that people can converse easily and that food can be passed around without obstruction.

These steps don't require strict Emily Post–style etiquette, but they let you bring out your personal style, layering textures and colors that feel right to you. It's all about blending elegance with the kind of comfort that makes everyone feel welcome.

My Must-Have List

- Poo-Pourri in every guest bathroom
- Fun guest towels. I love a seasonal towel, and these are fairly inexpensive at HomeGoods or T.J. Maxx.
- Paper products, like festive plates and napkins. Sophistiplate and Meri Meri are my go-to for seasonal paper products.
- I have three trays—a large, a medium, and a long rectangle—that I use for just about everything. They are white, easy to clean, inexpensive, and they are perfect for anything I need, from donuts to the Friendsgiving turkey.
- Throw blankets. I prefer the knit and woven blankets rather than chenille or cotton. I find knit

Table Tips

blankets are a bit more sturdy and hold up a little better in the wash.
- Scented candles. Hello, Capri Blue Volcano candle. The Better Homes & Gardens Red Lava Citrus candle is a total dupe on the Volcano candle, so try that one too.
- Sonos Move Bluetooth speaker. The JBL Flip speakers are also fantastic and can pair together, so you can have surround sound or the same music playing inside and outside.
- Extra universal phone chargers. Mine are already plugged in and ready to go in discreet areas throughout my house.
- Board games. They make any get-together last longer. Our favorites are Monopoly Deal, Ticket to Ride, and Codenames.

Helpful Hosting Accounts to Follow

- **@HomeWithHollyJ:** Holly brings a warm, approachable style to entertaining, focusing on attainable table décor, cozy recipes, and hosting tips that make guests feel welcomed.
- **@Simply2Moms:** AnnMarie and Anne share budget-friendly entertaining essentials from

Table Tips

simple serving pieces to DIY tablescape ideas, plus family-friendly recipes.
- **@ShopCreativeKitchen:** Jami is amazing and owns a shop about an hour from where I live. Her inspiration for entertaining, home décor, and functional tablescapes are so helpful and her tips are among the best out there.
- **@DishItGirlDina:** Not only does Dina have great recipes and supercute Instagram reels but she also has a podcast called *She Lives Fearless* that offers so much great inspiration.
- **@ShopSweetLulu:** Special occasions like Friendsgiving or Galentine's Day can be great ways to invite new people into your home. This account has all the inspiration you need for those fun holidays and everyday get-togethers.

Conversation Starter Resources

These resources will not only help in keeping the conversation flowing but also make your gatherings more enjoyable and memorable.

- **TableTopics Dinner Party:** This set includes 135 question cards designed to spark interesting conversations during meals. Each card features a

Table Tips

thought-provoking question, perfect for breaking the ice.

- **Serving with a Heart Like Jesus Conversation Starters:** This set is only available on Mardel's website. It includes twenty double-sided cards featuring questions aimed at sparking meaningful discussions, perfect for both spiritual and general topics.
- **TableTopics Family:** This set includes cards designed to initiate conversations during family meals, helping you create a natural rhythm around the table.
- **Faithful Hearts Couples Conversation Deck:** This resource from Christian Planner includes twelve different categories of questions, and while it says it's for couples, these are great questions to use to create thought-provoking conversations with anyone at your table.
- **Lumitory Legacy Conversation Cards:** This deck is designed to spark memories between kids, parents, and grandparents. With seventy-five questions, the cards help families connect over dinner or casual hangouts and connect over shared experiences.
- **Holy Quest Bible Trivia Game:** This is a fun, faith-based card game that helps friends and family explore deep topics, share personal stories, and strengthen connections, all while learning the Bible a little bit better.

Table Tips

Hospitality 101

When hosting guests at your home, there are several steps you can take to help everyone feel comfortable and welcome in your space.

- **Create a designated area for belongings:** Set up a specific spot for guests to place their coats, bags, and purses. This helps keep the entryway organized and makes guests feel more at ease.
- **Prepare the bathrooms:** In addition to a quick wipe-down, put out extra toilet paper and seasonal napkins and light a candle for a cozy atmosphere. These small touches show your guests that you thought about them.
- **Adjust the temperature:** Keeping the environment cozy is essential. If your home tends to be cool, consider having a basket of blankets accessible. Adjust the thermostat a few degrees to ensure your guests are comfortable.
- **Offer drinks thoughtfully:** Don't just provide a beverage upon arrival; have to-go cups ready for guests who might like a drink for the road. A handy tip is to ask local restaurants, like Chick-fil-A, for extra cups.
- **Set the mood with music:** Background music is essential for creating a festive atmosphere.

219

Table Tips

A system like Sonos allows you to play music throughout your home, enhancing the overall experience.

- **Engage guests upon arrival:** Have an immediate task for guests to do as they enter. This could be filling out a prayer card, grabbing a drink, or showing them to a guest room. Having a purpose helps guests settle in and feel more at home.
- **Prepare to-go containers:** At the end of the evening, have containers ready for guests to take leftovers home. Friends often appreciate this gesture, and it makes it easier for everyone to help tidy up.

When hosting overnight guests, here are some of my favorite touches to enhance their experience in the guest room:

- **Provide convenient power sources:** Ensure there are easily accessible outlets in the guest room, and consider placing a charging brick or power strip on the bedside table for their devices.
- **Prepare activities for kids:** Have a few engaging activities ready for younger guests, such as coloring books or small games, to keep them entertained during downtime.
- **Create a welcome basket:** Put together a thoughtful welcome basket for your guests that includes snacks, bottled water, fuzzy socks, and travel-sized toiletries for their convenience.

- **Stock the bathroom:** Make sure the bathroom is well-equipped with extra toilet paper, towels, and essentials like travel toothpaste, an extra toothbrush, or a razor to make their stay comfortable.
- **Make Wi-Fi information readily available:** Display the Wi-Fi password in a visible location, such as a frame near the front door, in the guest room, or in another prominent area of the house so guests can easily connect.

I hope you feel empowered and inspired to embrace the responsibility of hospitality with confidence. Remember, hosting isn't just about the food or the décor; it's about creating a space where relationships can flourish. It's about sharing love, laughter, and meaningful conversations that reflect the heart of Jesus. Each gathering is an opportunity to bless others, share your story, and reflect the joy of Christ in your life.

As you begin this journey of deepening your relationship with Jesus through consistent and meaningful hospitality, remember that it's okay to start small and learn as you go. Every get-together, dinner, or party will bring new experiences, and with each gathering you'll grow more comfortable in your ability to open your home and invite others in. So don't shy away from the

Table Tips

discomfort; embrace the moments to grow and learn alongside your people.

I pray that you feel encouraged to open your door wide and fill every seat the Lord has blessed you with. May your heart overflow with joy as you embrace the wonderful spirit of hospitality. Each gathering is a beautiful chance to deepen your relationship with Christ as we share our lives, love, and laughter together. Remember, it's not about the details or the perfect presentation; it's about the beautiful conversations and connections you create. So invite others in, cherish the journey of fellowship, and just let the biscuits burn.

Acknowledgments

GrandMary, you are the matriarch of our "little" family, and I'm so thankful to have such a sweet example of what it means to live a hospitable life. From having meals prepared hot and ready the moment people enter your home to living life with your door wide-open, your welcoming spirit leaves a legacy that will touch, and has touched, generations.

GrandMolly, you set the standard of hospitality above the rest, making everyone feel like they always have a seat at your table. Your desire to still cook a from-scratch meal for your family at age ninety-one is what having a heart for hospitality looks like, and I'm blessed to have such an authentic example of a true heart for serving others.

Kyle, late nights and early mornings in postpartum life made this book no small feat, but you stood by me with unwavering love and support. Your belief in what God is

Acknowledgments

doing through me carried me through the hardest chapters. Thank you for loving me selflessly, cheering me on, and reminding me I was never alone. I'm endlessly grateful to do life with you.

Mom, thank you for loving and serving our little family of three so well during those first six months postpartum while I was writing this book. From the meals you made, to the pep talks during hard phone calls, to all the sweet snuggles with John Maverick—every bit of it meant the world to me.

Carly, thank you for always being just a phone call away and for believing in this message from the very beginning. Here's to the first book of many.

Brigitta, your steady encouragement and thoughtful edits helped bring clarity and strength to these pages. I'm so grateful to have had your wisdom shaping this message.

Praise God from whom all blessings flow. All Glory to him forever.

Notes

Introduction
1. *Martha*, directed by R. J. Cutler (Netflix, 2024).

Chapter 2: Unpacking Hospitality
1. Martha Stewart, *Entertaining* (Clarkson Potter, 1982), chap. 1, Apple Books.
2. Matt Chandler, "Hospitality Is Courageous," The Gospel Coalition, April 13, 2018, https://www.thegospelcoalition.org/article/hospitality-courageous/.
3. Richard Kearney, "In the Wager: The Fivefold Motion," *Anatheism: Returning to God After God* (Columbia University Press, 2010): 40–56, https://www.jstor.org/stable/10.7312/kear14788.7.

Chapter 3: The Spiritual Discipline of Hospitality
1. Annie F. Downs, host, *That Sounds Fun with Annie F. Downs*, podcast, episode 429, "John Mark Comer on Spiritual Formation," That Sounds Fun Network, January 9, 2023, https://www.anniefdowns.com/podcast/episode-429-john-mark-comer-on-spiritual-formation/.
2. Jeffrey M. Schwartz, "Neuroplasticity and Spiritual Formation," *The Table*, April 18, 2019, https://cct.biola.edu/neuroplasticity-and-spiritual-formation/.

Notes

   3. James Clear, *Atomic Habits: An Easy and Proven Way to Build Good Habits and Break Bad Ones* (Avery, 2018), 50–51.

Chapter 4: Preparing Your Heart

   1. A. W. Tozer, *Whatever Happened to Worship?: A Call to True Worship* (WingSpread, 2012), chap. 4, Apple Books.
   2. Robert Robinson, "Come, Thou Fount of Every Blessing," 1758, Hymnary, accessed January 22, 2025, https://hymnary.org/text/come_thou_fount_of_every_blessing.
   3. Tim Chester, *A Meal with Jesus: Discovering Grace, Community, and Mission Around the Table* (Crossway, 2011), chap. 4, Apple Books.
   4. John Piper, "What Is the Will of God and How Do We Know It?," Desiring God, August 22, 2004, https://www.desiringgod.org/messages/what-is-the-will-of-god-and-how-do-we-know-it.
   5. John Piper, "What Is the Will of God and How Do We Know It?," sermon, posted April 4, 2013, by Desiring God, YouTube, 44:51, https://www.youtube.com/watch?v=06F4ru_tEw0.

Chapter 5: The Excuse You're Making

   1. Merrit Kennedy, "U.K. Now Has a Minister for Loneliness," NPR, January 17, 2018, https://www.npr.org/sections/thetwo-way/2018/01/17/578645954/u-k-now-has-a-minister-for-loneliness.
   2. UK Department of Health and Social Care et al., "New Every Mind Matters Campaign to Improve People's Mental Health," Gov.uk, October 5, 2021, https://www.gov.uk/government/news/new-every-mind-matters-campaign-to-improve-peoples-mental-health.

Chapter 6: Go Ahead and Let the Biscuits Burn

   1. Oswald Chambers, "Partakers of His Sufferings" in *My Utmost for His Highest* (Dodd, Mead, 1935), s.v. "November 5," archived at My Utmost for His Highest, accessed February 7, 2025, https://utmost.org/classic/partakers-of-his-sufferings-classic.
   2. "Wabi-Sabi: The Japanese Art of Finding the Beauty in Imperfections," Carnegie Library of Pittsburgh, accessed January 30, 2025, https://www.carnegielibrary.org/staff-picks/wabi-sabi-the-japanese-art-of-finding-the-beauty-in-imperfections.
   3. Curt Thompson, *Anatomy of the Soul: Surprising Connections Between Neuroscience and Spiritual Practices That Can Transform Your Life and Relationships* (Tyndale, 2010), chap. 1, Apple Books.

Notes

Chapter 7: The Intentional Invitation
1. "Early Christians and the Plague," Midtown Fellowship, March 18, 2020, https://midtowncolumbia.com/blog/early-christians-and-the-plague.
2. *Merriam-Webster Dictionary*, s.v. "invitation," accessed January 31, 2025, https://www.merriam-webster.com/dictionary/invitation.

Chapter 8: Habitual Hospitality
1. A. W. Tozer, *The Pursuit of God* (Christian Publications, 1948), 91.
2. David T. Neal et al., "Habits—A Repeat Performance," *Current Directions in Psychological Science* 15, no. 4: 198–202, https://doi.org/10.1111/j.1467-8721.2006.00435.x.
3. Praxis, "The Rule in One Page," A Rule of Life for Redemptive Entrepreneurs, accessed February 7, 2025, PDF, https://rule.praxislabs.org/wp-content/uploads/2019/11/ROL-in-one-page.pdf.

Chapter 9: The Great Invite
1. Skip Heitzig, "Full Service 9/8/2024: Prayer: It's Not Just for Sundays—James 5:13-16," streamed live by Calvary Church with Skip Heitzig, YouTube, September 8, 2024, 1:37:18, https://www.youtube.com/watch?v=FbRC71Lk7_g.

Chapter 10: Serving Others Without Burning Out
1. Allie Beth Stuckey, cover copy to *You're Not Enough (And That's Okay): Escaping the Toxic Culture of Self-Love* (Sentinel, 2020).
2. Stuckey, cover copy to *You're Not Enough*.
3. Christine D. Pohl, *Making Room: Recovering Hospitality as a Christian Tradition* (Eerdmans, 1999), 130.
4. Pohl, *Making Room*, 128.

Chapter 11: The Legacy of Your Table
1. Pohl, *Making Room*, chap. 8, Apple Books.
2. Amy White (@hi.im.amywhite), "WAFFLES at 10 TRADITION," Instagram, August 26, 2023, https://www.instagram.com/reel/Cwa4BpSs04E/?igsh=MWs4YWtrMXR5d3RqcQ%3D%3D.
3. Dustin Willis and Brandon Clements, *The Simplest Way to Change the World: Biblical Hospitality as a Way of Life* (Moody, 2017), 46.

About the Author

Abby Turner Kuykendall is a newly married thirty-something who grew up in a home that taught her marriage is what happens after you graduate. But after graduating from Ouachita Baptist University, she went to graduate school at Baylor—single and mourning every sense of the word. That led her to discover the power of the table in building a flourishing, God-centered community. Over the next five years, Abby developed her love of food, photography, and human behavior. This ultimately led her to begin her blog, *A Table Top Affair*. While Abby found her stride in her corporate career, she found meaningful purpose around her table, which led her to write her debut cookbook, *The Living Table*. Abby lives with her husband, Kyle, in northwest Arkansas. They welcomed their son, John Maverick, in April 2024.